HOW TO
SELL
WHEN NOBODY'S
BUYING

HOW TO
SELL
WHEN NOBODY'S
BUYING

(AND HOW TO SELL EVEN

MORE WHEN THEY ARE)

DAVE LAKHANI

WILEY

John Wiley & Sons, Inc.

ISBN: 978-0470-50489-5

Printed in the United States of America

10 9 8 7 6 5 4 3 2 1

First and always foremost:
To Austria Raine Lakhani
My sweet daughter, my good friend,
my partner in crime, and my best teacher.
And to some of the other teachers
in my life—you've made
all the difference for me:
Dr. Rachna Jain
Dr. Kalinda Rose Stevenson
James Hunter
Shawn Lee
Joel Bauer

And finally, to every salesperson
who picks up this book and implements
what he learns: I'm honored
to be a part of your success.

CONTENTS

ACKNOWLEDGMENTS

I could write a whole book of acknowledgments and I'd still miss someone.

I'd like to thank Dr. Rachna Jain for help with edits and for doing what every good psychologist does: listen while I'm ranting and then laugh … at least I think that is what good psychologists do. Anyway, it worked for me.

I'd like to thank my brother Bill Willard for keeping things going while I was writing. You are a great asset and an inspiration. I hope to become half the explorer you are.

I want to thank virtually every person who has purchased something from me, from the time I started selling *Grit* newspaper at age 7 or 8 to you reading this book. You've created the experience that has allowed me to share with so many people, and I thank you.

This book wouldn't be nearly as good as it is without the contributing authors who are subject matter specialists on some very important topics that you need to know about. So thank you for your contributions, Ray Cronise, Dr. Rachna Jain, Mari Smith, and Craig Ernst.

I'd also like to thank Todd Carlson, Dwayne Speagle, Joel Bauer, Scott Marker, Michael Lovitch, and everyone on Twitter,

Facebook, and LinkedIn who asked me questions for the book or who shared their thoughts and insights. I appreciate all of you.

To everyone who follows me on Twitter, "friends" me on Facebook, connects with me on LinkedIn, or buys a book or program from me: I'm thrilled that you have enough respect for me to invest the time, effort, and headspace it takes to consume my message. You mean the world to me.

To Gail Kingsbury, Kevin Hogan, Heather Porter, Donna Fox, Ben Mack, Harv Eker, Stephen Pierce, Tony Robbins, Seth Godin, Chet Holmes, Chris Howard, Bill Braseth, Rod Schlienz, Ted Goodier, David Bassiri, Mike Willard, and all my friends in The Entrepreneur's Organization around the world, especially those in my forum, I appreciate you.

Special thanks to Joel Bauer, who always brings me back to focus with the question, "How do you sell it, and what is the profit?" Thanks Joel, you've become an amazing friend. Let's go skiing!

To Dr. John Stukey and Tara, thanks for all the laughs when I was writing and not laughing much!

Finally to all my clients and students, thank you for going out and selling anyway, even when everyone says nobody is buying. You guys get it and your bank accounts prove it.

PREFACE

Selling changed and someone forgot to tell the sales teams.
—Dave Lakhani

That quote is an interesting way to start a book about how to sell when nobody's buying. That quote, combined with rapidly changing economic conditions, is the basis for why nobody's buying.

Twentieth-century selling techniques are dead, but salespeople are trying to ignore its rotting corpse in boardrooms and business lunches around the world every hour of every day. It's time to face the facts: If you want to sell and succeed today, you have to update your skills. The techniques your sales manager learned in a seminar in 1974 that were based on tactics developed in 1954 aren't going to help you today. You must develop new strategies and new tactics that reflect the reality of these times—our times. This book will help you do that, but you have to be open to the idea that you are going to work harder and learn more than you have in the past so that you can thrive in the future. If you can't commit to learning something new, no matter how long you've been selling, you should simply quit now; selling isn't for you anymore. Walk away with your dignity intact and find a new career.

If, however, you are willing to buckle down, to learn and test some new ideas in your industry (yes, yours; it is just like everyone else's), then selling when nobody's buying is your time to succeed.

Ask yourself this question: Is it really true that nobody's buying? Of course it's not. Economies change, businesses come and go, but what is more accurate is to say that the same people you are used to selling to might not be buying. The people you've always relied on for sales might not be buying. But someone is. You might not even be able to find buyers by looking in the same places you've always looked, but they are still out there. However, you certainly won't find them using the same old tools you've always used.

From the 1980s onward, armed with big budgets, venture capital, and, for the most part, a buzzing economy, sales changed. Big salaries were available; lofty titles such as chief sales officer were offered up, and VP of sales titles were handed out to anyone who showed up, whether they had five minutes of management experience or not. In many industries, sales happened without a lot of work; you simply had to show up to sell. The selling process changed. Salespeople were no longer experts, they were sales professionals; the experts came with them to demonstrate and to answer tough questions, the account managers came behind them to build the relationship, but the salespeople sat in the middle, selling ... sort of. You see, in times of big budgets, you need only show up to sell, but when nobody's buying you have to do something different. That is what this book is all about. I'll go so far as to argue that after 2009 the world of business and consumer buying will be a fundamentally different place, one that will require a completely different mindset and a different kind of salesperson to succeed.

Modern salespeople must arm themselves with a new set of skills. They must not only flex with their environment, the economy, and their company; they must also assimilate and adapt new skills to meet people where they live and work. The Internet has changed a lot of things, including how we sell and how we buy.

The skills you are about to learn will not only help you sell when nobody's buying—they'll be the core skills you need to compete in 2009 and beyond.

0

QUICK START

HOW TO SELL MORE RIGHT NOW

No matter what, there are always more people who want to buy, always.

—Dave Lakhani

I get it. You are in a slump, times are hard, and your industry is going sideways; the economy sucks. Whatever is going on has caused you to need to increase sales—and fast. So this chapter is about what you can do when the chips are down to create new sales very quickly while you build on the new strategies that I'll teach you in the rest of the book. But right now let's get focused on some high-value, high-impact actions that you can take.

WARNING!

If you find yourself saying "Yeah, yeah" or "I already know this," then I'll respectfully submit that the problem with sales isn't the economy or anything else; it is you. When you are slumping, you go to things that work consistently. Some of them may not be fun (I'll save those for later in the book), and some

---

may require you to work harder than you've had to in the past. And I only have one response to that:

Get over it!

That's right, you don't need to be coddled right now; that isn't going to get you any closer to the sales you need. You need hard, actionable information that you can start using today. So let's get to it.

SEVEN DAYS TO SELLING SUCCESSFULLY WHEN NOBODY'S BUYING

Day One

No cold calling today. Ha! You thought I was going to tell you to make calls to a bunch of new prospects, but I'm not . . . not yet, anyway. Instead I want you to follow these instructions:

- Call 25 clients from your inactive client list. Talk to them about engaging with you again. If they are inactive because of issues with the company, get someone busy, including you, resolving the issue if it will lead to a sale. Ask them the question, "If I could get this resolved right away, would you have a conversation about moving forward together again?" If the answer is yes, get busy. If the answer is no, send the problem to someone who can resolve it and get him on the case; your clients may change their minds once their problem is solved.
- Call 10 of your existing clients and don't ask them if they would consider buying something additional from you; instead, present them with an offer. Sell them an upgrade, an additional service, a new product. Have a plan and pitch. I don't care if they bought from you last week and you know they'll say no; call anyway.
- Call someone who is not a competitor but supplies complementary products or services to clients like yours, and

tell them you have five great clients you'd be willing to introduce them to and endorse them if they'll do the same. If they say no, keep calling until you get someone smart enough to say yes. Then, when they say yes, turn to Chapter 7 to see how to set up the whole process.

- For the hour before you leave the office tonight, review the action plan for tomorrow and get everything you need in place so that you can hit the ground running. Create a list of 10 people you can ask for referrals, 5 people you can ask for a testimonial, and 20 people who've asked for more information but to whom you haven't spoken in the past 10 days. I also want you to get the names and addresses of 10 prospects you'd like to be doing business with.
- Make all your client follow-up and prospect calls today, before you leave the office.
- Just before you walk out the door, sit back down and leave five voice mails for people who've requested information in the past month and tell them that you'll be calling them tomorrow because you discovered something important that will impact them.

By the way, I don't care if you sell doughnuts, diamonds, or document processing—the rules are the same, no excuses.

Day Two

Today is going to be busy again; you need to turn up the focus. If you found yourself getting distracted, today is not the day for that. Stick with me; this is easier than a diet. Massive focused activity leads to massive results, so here we go!

Call 10 people who could give you a referral and say this specifically; don't cheat, read it. "Hi, <*insert name*>, I'm calling because it is a tough time in our industry and I wanted to know who I could refer to you right now that would help your business grow. As you know, I talk to a lot of people every day, and I want to be able to send you some good referrals." Listen, take notes, and then if you know someone right away who would be a good fit, give him or her one referral on the spot. If you don't know anyone off the top of your head, that is okay, too. Then say, "Because these are such odd times, I'm wondering if you'd mind doing me a favor, too. Who do you know that would be a good fit to work with me? Someone like you who has the same sort of needs you do, or someone who you know would be an exceptional fit. Is there anyone like that you could refer me to now, while I'm searching for a referral for you?" Then wait for a response.

Now, the caveat here is that you really do need to try and give them a referral as well, so don't call on people that you know you wouldn't feel comfortable referring others to. When you call their referral, you are going to say to the gatekeeper or on voice mail, "*<Insert name of person who referred you>* said he respected you and that you'd be a good person to ask a question about using *<insert your product>*." Then move into your pitch.

One of the big things that costs you time during the day is all the little things that you need to do: appointments to get the car serviced, finding addresses and phone numbers for prospects, all that stuff. I want you to take a brief break and go to www.asksunday.com right now and sign up for a free trial for one of their personal assistants; then I want you to dump off all the stuff you have to do the rest of the week that someone else can do for you. Need an oil change? Let them find someone to come to you to do it, and while they're at it, ask them to find a coupon, if there is one. Let them do it. I'm serious about this; give yourself a break. If you need to research something, have them do it and give you their compiled research. Your time is more valuable focused on selling. Be creative with how you use these guys; they can take a lot of the burden off you and help you be much more productive.

It's time to call those people who've asked you for information but with whom you haven't followed up within the past 10 days. Call each and every one of them and either talk to them and move them forward or disqualify them. If they are not available, leave them a voice mail with one strong, compelling reason to call back . . . and leave them two times; you'll try them back once today and once tomorrow. I know that this is going to be a challenge for you. There is a reason you haven't followed up with these people in the past 10 days; maybe it was because you didn't think they were interested or because you just haven't gotten around to it. Whatever the issue, get it done. Where there is fuel, there is the potential for fire, so make the calls.

Once that is done, you are going to call five people you can ask for testimonials—people who are thrilled to be working with you and who are willing to say so. Your goal is to convert all of them and get them to agree to doing the testimonial. Ideally, you'd like to have it on video, but that may not be practical, so go to www.conferencetown.com and sign up for a free conference call line. There you'll be able to record their testimonials as an MP3 that you can e-mail as an attachment to other prospects, put on your web site, and include on a CD that you send out later. It is more impactful than a written testimonial because the listener can get more dimension from it; it is a real person speaking about your product. You can also transcribe it and put the written portion up on your web site, and you can send your referrers the text and ask them if they'd mind putting it on their corporate letterhead as well. Now you've got a powerful testimonial to use on all your future calls.

It's time to set up 10 prospects that you'd really like to do business with, to get them to take your call and do business with you. First, go to Starbucks and buy 10 $5 coffee cards. If you need approval from someone to buy the cards, show them this book and this quick-start guide and tell them that you are following it step by step, verbatim, and that you'd like to get the cards.

If they won't buy them, I want you to strongly consider buying them yourself. If you can't afford $50 right now, then feel free to only buy five cards, but that is the very minimum. You are going to create a letter that says the following:

Dear <insert prospect name>,

I'm sending you a one-page letter because I'd like to earn your business. I'm sending you a Starbucks card because I want to help you think; more about that in a minute. I made this letter only one page so you could hear me out quickly. I only want one thing: a chance to talk to you on the phone for exactly seven minutes. Before you say yes, I want to share three ways I think my company can help you, and I'd like you to think about them:

<Insert three bullet points about how you can help them>

<Insert one testimonial from a high-visibility client>

I look forward to having an opportunity to talk to you in the coming week. When I call I'd like to schedule a time on your calendar; if you'll let your assistant know I'm calling, I'll book everything with her, or if you book your own appointments, I'll be courteous, professional, and brief, schedule the appointment with you, and wait to talk on the appointed day.

I get some of my best thinking done in the morning with my first cup of coffee, tea, or hot chocolate (depending on the mood); it just seems to help. And I just found out that caffeine stimulates thoughtfulness and creativity. Anyway, I wanted you to have a beverage on me in the morning as you consider my proposal. I'll be calling on <insert a date after which you know they'll have gotten the letter> to schedule our appointment. If you'd like to contact me earlier, here is my cell phone number; call me any time it is convenient for you and we'll schedule the appointment or talk right then.

Best regards,

<Insert your name and cell phone number>

Now, do the following:

- Make all your client follow-up and prospect calls today, before you leave.
- Get prepared for tomorrow; you have a big day ahead of you. You'll need the name of three local prospects that you've been trying to reach and the contact info for 10 prospects who said no to your proposal in the past 90 days. You need to leave for work early tomorrow, so get a good night's sleep.

Day Three

Bring a pair of scissors to work with you today. On your way to work you are going to stop at a store and buy some scotch tape and a roll of two-inch-wide red, blue, or purple ribbon and three matching bows. You are then going to go to the local doughnut shop and buy three dozen doughnuts, a dozen in each of three boxes. Then:

- Wrap the ribbon around the doughnut box once the long way, top to bottom; cut it and tape the ends to the box so you have a nice flat piece of ribbon around the top and down the sides of the box, taped to the box on the bottom. You'll now repeat the process with your second piece of ribbon, this time side to side, creating a cross on the top of the box. In the center of the cross you'll place one bow. Do that to all three boxes.
- You'll now drive each box of doughnuts to each prospect's office. Walk in with the wrapped box of doughnuts and announce that you have a personal delivery for your prospect. Ask if the prospect could come to the front so you can give him or her the delivery. When he or she arrives, deliver the doughnuts and introduce yourself. Then say, "I've been trying to reach you and haven't had

any luck; I was worried I'd been too gruff, so I thought I'd take the sweet approach. I figured you and your team might enjoy the doughnuts. I don't want to take a lot of your time right now, but I'd like to schedule an appointment to talk to you on the phone this week. Which day could we schedule?" Then wait for the answer. He may be willing to talk to you right then, or he may want to schedule the appointment; take either option. Leave him with any collateral material you feel is appropriate.

- When you get back to the office, you'll call 10 prospects who didn't buy from you. They may have purchased from someone else or they may have decided not to buy. Your job is to find out if what they bought instead of your product is serving them well or if they are still in need of what you sell.

- The rest of the day is devoted to writing a 500- to 800-word article that you will submit online. Write the article and submit it at www.ezine.com; be sure to include your name, a brief bio, and a link back to your web site so people who are searching for information in your category can contact you. The key to the article is to write about something timely and topical, showing how your product or service is solving a problem a lot of people in your industry are having.

- Make all your client follow-up and prospect calls today, before you leave.

- Plan your schedule for tomorrow by making a list of the top 25 sales that, if you could make them, would make your whole year, maybe more. Write those down; tomorrow you'll need them.

Day Four

- Today you are going to research your top 25 prospects. I want you to read everything you can find about these companies on their web sites, Google them, call any vendors you know and where you have contacts who work with them, and get any insights you can. I want you to spend the day today becoming a subject matter expert on your top 25 prospects.

- Make a list next to each of the prospect's names of ways you can help them based on what you've found. Include creative ways of connecting with them as well as interesting tidbits you can use to open the conversation and any other material you find useful.
- Gather the contact information for each of the prospects so that you can start contacting them in earnest on Monday.
- Make all your client follow-up and prospect calls today, before you leave.
- Prepare for tomorrow; finish the week hard.

Day Five

Finishing the week hard is the sign of a true champion. When your competition is preparing for the weekend, I want you to turn on the juice; you'll have time to cool down over the weekend. Remember, the home stretch is where winners win while losers quit. Now:

- Call five satisfied customers and ask them about other ways you might be of assistance. Talk to them about other products or services you have, and discuss how they might integrate them. Ask them what else you can do to support them, and be willing to pitch in and help.
- Pay off at least three referral exchanges. Give people who gave you a referral a referral in return.
- Do your research and try to find two networking leads, groups, or events that you can attend in the next 10 days where prospects will be. Schedule yourself to attend.

- If you haven't already used all your asksunday.com tasks, give them something to do for you over the weekend that will save you time or make you more productive next week.
- Write five thank-you letters to people who have purchased from you recently.
- Make all your client follow-up and prospect calls today, before you leave.
- Plan next week's activities.
- Congratulate yourself and reward yourself for following this plan all week (if you really did)—go out for a nice dinner, do something you enjoy, and know that you made a solid effort this week.

If you've followed this quick-start plan for a whole week and done everything that I've outlined for you, you'll have created tremendous momentum. That momentum is what it takes to make sales when times are challenging.

This quick-start guide will give you the emotional energy to do the rest of the processes in the book that will make you successful when everyone else struggles. The only material in this book that doesn't work is the material you don't implement.

The fastest way to improve yourself and your sales is to focus more; do one thing extra every day and be willing to step outside your box. If you do, you'll find more success than about 99% of the rest of the salespeople working today. The only thing standing between you and your next sale is you.

Now let's get into the really good stuff so that you can systematically improve your game!

1

GET REAL AND
GET FOCUSED

Economies and industries change; that's not your fault. But responding to the change profitably is your responsibility.
— Dave Lakhani

You likely picked up this book because you are experiencing a sales slump of some sort. It could be caused by the economy or a change in your industry, or maybe a run of bad days. Whatever it is, I want you to know right now that you can change your results, and it won't take a long time.

This chapter is about reality, how you think, and how you work. You'll be tempted to skip this chapter and go right to the sections that have tactics that you can use. I'll caution you not to do that, because if you do you'll be missing one of the biggest lessons in how to overcome any economy and any slump. And the hidden lesson here is that being thorough, being complete, and taking all the steps are what lead to success in learning and in sales.

One thing every professional salesperson can be sure of is that throughout their careers, many things will change; there will be exceptionally good times, very average times, and some really tough times. This is the nature of sales. Economies change, industries change, buyers change, and the most successful salespeople are able to react quickly, learn what they need to succeed, and take action. When it comes to selling in challenging times, implementation is everything, and money follows action. If you choose to sit around and think the sky is falling, you'll miss the many opportunities that show up that didn't exist when just anyone could show up and get a sale. Challenging times hone you to a fine edge that makes you effective and profitable when others struggle, and that allows you to prosper even more in the good times.

WHEN NOBODY'S BUYING, PEOPLE BECOME PREDICTABLE

When economies or industries change, sales managers begin chanting their predictable mantra: "You just need to cold call more, push people harder, cut back on your expenses; no more client dinners or paying for golf." If simply cold calling new prospects and cutting back on client entertainment were the answer, there would never be a lack of sales. But with changing economies, with changing access to information, with changing and consolidating industries, sales strategies have to change, too . . . yet they've remained fundamentally the same for years.

When economies and industries change, CEOs, vice presidents, and buyers of all kinds begin chanting their own mantra: "We have to make across-the-board cuts, make do with the technology we have, cut back on all spending, negotiate everything, and put a hold on all contracts until we see what is really going to happen."

And with that, salespeople pick up the phone and start cold calling, trying desperately to reach buyers directly who they've never spoken to before—and buyers develop more sophisticated strategies for avoiding their calls. Companies struggle to meet revenue projections, and salespeople wonder if they should look for greener pastures. Business continues to stagnate and decline.

But it doesn't have to.

You are about to learn what works today; you are going to learn how to think differently and to act differently so that you can always sell when nobody's buying and sell even more when they are.

There are two trains of thought about selling in tough times. The first is that times are not tough, it is really all in your head and you just need to work harder and with a better attitude to sell more. It is tough to accept that argument when the businesses you sell to no longer exist or when a major change in your industry or the economy causes people to behave differently. The second line of thought is that the sky is falling; everything is bad no matter where you look. Don't waste a lot of time trying to sell anything, no one is buying anyway. It is time to commiserate with others who feel the same way; they understand. Listen to the media for very long in any economic change and you'll soon be convinced that the apocalypse is on your heels and the only thing to do is bury your head in the sand and wait for the inevitable . . . whatever it is.

Reality, however, is something different. Difficult, challenging times offer unique opportunities for smart salespeople to make more sales than they ever have before and to position themselves for extreme success when the cycles change. Selling when nobody is buying requires a different approach, not the one that your sales manager learned in 1974 or even the sales techniques you learned a year or two ago—it requires that you learn some new but very simple skills that will allow you to dominate the current marketplace, no matter what the condition. It also requires that you do even more of what you are doing well. The exciting part is that as the marketplace changes, you'll constantly be evolving on the front edge of the change, not in the back, where all the competition is. Before I get further into that idea, let's take a look at business cycles.

Dr. Clement Jugular (1819–1905) was one of the first to develop the idea of a business cycle. His work led to many more advanced business and economic cycle discoveries and definitions. For salespeople, his initial business cycle description is probably the most useful in terms of thinking about selling. The four cycles according to Jugular are:

1. Expansion
2. Prosperity
3. Contraction
4. Recession

In the current economy (2009) we've seen wholesale devastation of the housing market, bailout of banks, economic stimulus packages that really did nothing, and businesses and jobs disappearing at record rates. I think most people would agree that we are in Stage 4, recession.

And that is the best time to sell.

In recessionary times, several things happen. Many people steer away from sales jobs, leaving the market ripe for the picking. Even more salespeople believe that no one is buying because the techniques they've always used aren't working, so they stick their heads in the sand and do nothing. Coincidently, I believe it is precisely what salespeople do that kicks off Stage 1, expansion.

Entrepreneurs and entrepreneurial salespeople get hungry; they go out, they find and sell solutions, they create opportunities in the vacuums left by others' exits. They take massive, focused action. The result is nothing less than expansion in industries where these pockets of revolutionary thinking exist, where people like you create the future. They do whatever it takes to be successful. They ask their clients what they can do to help, and then they get busy doing it. The law of reciprocation says that people are much more likely to give you something when you've given them something first.

There is a gap between recession and expansion that is ripe for focused salespeople to really make their mark, and here's why: After the expansion phase has kicked off and is about halfway through its cycle, everyone jumps on the bandwagon and tries to grab what would appear to be low-hanging fruit. Everyone loves to sell in the good times. They see opportunity everywhere because the economy is flourishing. But in the space covering recession and expansion is real opportunity for those salespeople who think better, work smarter, and try harder. Those salespeople create expansion and they reap the rewards. This book is all about how to leverage that time as well as how to position yourself to sell even more in the expansion and prosperity periods.

The great news about economic cycles is that the good times last a lot longer than the bad times. Since the great depression of the 1930s we've had a good number of setbacks in the economy, and we've consistently recovered faster from each successive one. Where recovery took almost a decade after the Great Depression, we've recovered from most recent economic slumps in a few years or less. The same is true of your industry, unless you are in an industry that is truly going away; the need for your product or service will return to the masses more quickly.

REALITY IS WHAT YOU FACE EVERY DAY

I've noticed that no matter how good times are, there are a lot of salespeople who can't sell, and when times are hard there are a lot of salespeople who are getting rich. And as you've probably heard before, whether you think you can or think you can't, you are right. And boy, would it be nice if it were that easy.

For exceptional salespeople, reality is not simply looking at what is happening in the economy or in the market. Reality involves, in fact, taking in everything that is happening in your industry, in your market, and in your company and developing a powerful plan for leveraging that material in your favor to help your prospects while getting what you need as well. The question that will arise is: "How do I do that?" And the answer is quite simple.

YOU DO WHATEVER IT TAKES

As I travel around the world training salespeople, I get the same question over and over: "What can I do to sell more now?" And the answer I'll give you is never the answer they want to hear. The answer is, you do whatever it takes to meet your quota and to get the sale. Of course, that doesn't give you permission to be unethical or untruthful, but it does give you permission to start thinking differently. I also tell salespeople that they need to take the time to learn what is working now.

Doing whatever it takes means just that—it means you dig deeper, you look harder, and you build relationships deeper and deeper in the organization. And your sales manager got it right: You make the extra calls, you call those people who are on your inactive list, you call new prospects, you call people who were doing business with you and left, you call old prospects you didn't close business with. Too many salespeople leave money on the table because they don't go back and talk to people who've raised their hands and asked for information, even if they didn't move forward before. But that is only part of the equation. You've also got to become an aggressive prospector who develops phenomenal skill at getting the appointment. A mistake many sales professionals make is asking this question: "What can I sell to people who have money to buy today?" The question they should be asking is, "How do I find the people who have a need and a capacity for buying the product I have to sell?" The difference is that flitting around trying to match products or services to people with money is a losing game and you'll never come out on top.

When nobody is buying, it is time to do whatever it takes to find the people who are, to learn new influence strategies to sell to the ones who are on the fence. It means that you have to get more creative than ever with the budget you have to reach the clients you need. It means working harder, longer, and often without immediate financial reward in order to achieve great success. The payoff in the long run is that as the economy changes or as your industry changes, you'll be on the front end of profitability from all the hard work you did today.

FOCUS IS THE REAL KEY TO MORE SALES

In an over-communicated, over-stimulated world, most people will tell you that they are able to effectively multitask and to focus. In reality, however, nothing is further from the truth. Study after study is beginning to emerge that demonstrates that the time lost in trying to focus when attempting to multitask is much greater than the time people believe multitasking saves.

I wrote a book called *The Power of an Hour* (Wiley, 2006) that looked at focus and how to apply it, across the board, to your life. I want to share a key concept from that book and I want you to apply it as you go through your day and even as you go through this book.

PRACTICE FEARSOME FOCUS USING THE
45/15 FORMULA

Fearsome focus™ is the single-minded ability to concentrate fully on the task at hand without allowing anything to impact your effort to perform that task. That means that you don't accept interruptions for any reason, that you don't do anything else, even for a second, while you are focused on the task. If you are calling prospects, no checking e-mail for even just a second, no looking something up on the Internet because it entered your mind, no idle chit-chat with people who just need a "quick second." Your focus is on calling prospects, connecting with prospects, and moving the sale forward—nothing else.

Fearsome focus works best for sales professionals who use the 45/15 formula. That means that you practice fearsome focus for 45 minutes, and then the bottom 15 minutes of the hour give you time to quickly check e-mail and voice-mail, do anything else you need, move around a little, and then get back to the next task.

For this process to work best, it is important that you condition the people around you to your new process and that you follow the process rigorously.

HOW TO CONDITION YOUR COLLEAGUES TO RESPECT YOUR FEARSOME FOCUS

1. Tell people that you are implementing a new plan for increasing sales and it requires all your attention for brief periods of time throughout the day. When you ask not to be interrupted, tell them you'd like them to support your commitment to increasing sales by not interrupting you until 45 minutes past the hour (or whenever your 45 minutes will end).

2. When people interrupt you (and they will), gently but firmly tell them that you are absolutely unavailable now but that you'll connect with them at 45 minutes past the hour (or whenever your 45 minutes end). Honor your commitment and follow up with people who need it.

3. Be consistent about your application of the process; try to schedule similar activities for the same time every day.

4. Condition your colleagues to expect to hear back from you on urgent e-mails at the bottom 15 minutes of the hour and non-urgent e-mails by the end of the business day.

5. Schedule times to talk to colleagues rather than dropping in; respect their time and focus as you ask them to respect yours.

To be successful with this process, you need to be sure that before beginning a task you have all your tools together to complete the task you are focusing on. Getting up to get something you forgot is not being in fearsome focus. Fearsome focus works because you can start the task and accomplish a significant amount without having to distract yourself for 5 or 10 minutes as you go looking for what you need.

SUGGESTED FEARSOME FOCUS ACTIVITIES

Prospecting. You should have at least one fearsome focus block per day focused only on prospecting. When I refer to *prospecting,* I mean making calls to set up appointments to talk, not to researching potential prospects; that should be done at a separate time.

E-mail. E-mail takes up a massive amount of time for most people during the day. My recommendation is that you become very aggressive about what e-mail you handle. If it doesn't require a response, don't send one. Set up a time at the end of the day and focus for 45 minutes on all your e-mail. You'll be shocked at how much more productive you become if you simply scan e-mail in your 15-minute downtimes and then move e-mails that need to be responded to into a Respond Tonight folder, then respond each evening. Client and prospect e-mails should always get a timely response if they need it when you are scanning, but if they don't require immediate response, they go to the Respond Tonight folder. I like doing this process in the evening rather than the middle of the day simply because there are e-mails that I don't want to leave hanging overnight.

Planning for tomorrow. Each day I suggest that you spend an hour in fearsome focus mode, planning your next day. That means getting your call list together so that you can get to work and immediately engage when you arrive at the office. Get any tools, information, or other material together the night before as well. Condition yourself to profitable action each morning when you arrive at your office and you'll be more profitably productive throughout the day.

Review. At least once a week, create a time to review this book and pull out ideas that you can implement in the coming week or with specific prospects. Use that time to discover what you can do differently than you've always done.

Schedule. Create a fearsome focus time for anything that you need to get done quickly and efficiently. The extent to which you follow this plan is the extent to which you'll succeed faster.

In later chapters of the book I'll describe things you can do that will allow you to maximize your effectiveness and increase the amount of time available to you as well. But for now I want you to focus on one thing at a time. *Focus, accomplish, relax, focus.* That is your new mantra for the coming days. As you begin using the process, you'll see what a better implementer you are becoming.

GET HELP: YOU DON'T HAVE TO DO EVERYTHING YOURSELF

I can do it faster and better myself are the fatal last words of the overwhelmed who never achieve their potential
— Dave Lakhani

In this chapter I talked about focus and how important it is. And focus will take you a very long way toward your goals. But as your focus increases, so does the need to get rid of low-value activities. Low-value activities are some of the biggest time wasters and distracters from your sales efforts. Here are some typical low-value activities:

- Scheduling personal appointments
- Excessive Internet research

- Data entry
- Quick follow-up calls that are not moving the sale forward
- Spending time on hold with customer service
- Scheduling travel
- Getting restaurant reservations
- Deleting spam from your e-mail
- Confirming, changing, or canceling appointments
- Filling out expense reports

The list could go on for pages. If you'll take a week and write down how much time you spend on unproductive activities, I think you'll be surprised. It isn't the hours that you give up that cost you profitable selling time; it is the little things that take "only" 10 minutes that you do dozens of times a week that kill your productivity.

PASS OFF WHAT YOU CAN TO SUPPORT STAFF YOU ALREADY HAVE

Nearly every organization has a set of support staff that can help you with certain tasks. I want you to see how many tasks you can either give or give back to other staff in your office right now.

If you've been doing things that support staff would normally do, you may get some pushback on your requests. This is where most people give up and utter the fatal, "It will be easier and faster if I do it myself." Don't do it. Stay committed and stick with it. Every task that someone else can do brings you one step closer to your next sale. You are not giving up things only you can do; you are giving up things that are stealing your profitable selling time. Every hour you gain back is an hour you can spend prospecting, speaking with prospects, managing clients, or working on other high-value activities.

A RADICAL APPROACH TO TAKING BACK
PRODUCTIVE TIME

I want you to become aggressive about taking back your time. Every minute you spend doing things that are low-value uses of your time is time you could be spending making a sale.

I want you to hire a virtual assistant. For $40 a month you can hire a personal assistant who will do basic simple tasks for you; for around $250 a month you can hire an assistant for 20 hours. These assistants are highly skilled at taking care of the administrative and life tasks that you waste time on. You can even try them for free for a week, and I want you to commit to doing this by going to www.asksunday.com and sign up for the free trial. Let them take care of several tasks for you this week and see how freeing it is. It costs you less than $13 an hour to have someone who will more than likely help you regain well over 20 hours per month. If that seems like too much, share the assistant with an officemate, your spouse, or a friend. Virtually anyone can find $125 a month to buy back time.

What could you do with an extra half a week a month? If you look at it as an eight-hour day, you are gaining nearly three full working days per month, or you are gaining three extra days with your family. You could nearly take off every Friday and still be as productive as you are today. Here are just a few of the things that your assistant can do for you:

- E-mail
- Update your customer relationship management (CRM) system
- Create spreadsheets
- Prospect research/other research
- Competitive data gathering
- Find requests for proposal (Raps)
- Get on the phone with customer service to solve issues for you

- Pay your bills
- Schedule your doctor, dental, vehicle, and other appointments
- Shop for presents for you
- Format documents, create PDF files
- Create process maps, flowcharts, and the like
- Proofread your documents and letters
- Do comparison shopping for you and give you the top three choices
- Upload content for your blog
- Maintain your Face book profile and respond to general requests
- Set up autopsy for all your bills
- Create your expense report

Again, the list of what an assistant can take off your plate goes on and on. If you'll spend only a little time thinking this through, you'll find many opportunities to take back your time.

When I was a VP of sales I found that one of the biggest causes of slumps was not the economy or industry upheavals; it was time spent on "busy work" and low-value activities. I also found that salespeople who had the highest job dissatisfaction were those who spent extra time at the office doing low-value work rather than spending that time with their families. When I did a time audit with them and pointed out the low-value activities that they could pass off to existing support staff, they were relieved. However, the big challenge was getting them to actually pass off those activities. They were so conditioned to believe that they can do these things better and faster that they wouldn't give them up. I suspect you'll initially have the same problem, too. The trick is to give up the things that you think matter least and to get the things done that you never quite get around to. In other words, give up things that don't really matter to you but that you do anyway, and get the nagging things done that you never get to. There is a great sense of freedom in giving up on things that don't matter and completing tasks that are occupying mind space.

THERE IS NO WAY I CAN AFFORD THIS

In the tiniest number of cases, it might actually be true that you can't afford what I'm suggesting, but rarely has anyone told me that they can't afford $40 a month for the most basic service or that it didn't save them tremendous time.

If you really can't afford it for whatever reason, consider getting an intern. Put together an outline of your requirements and take it to your local college to find out what it takes to get an intern at your company. Interns get valuable work experience and credit they need to graduate, and you get the assistance you need.

Also check at local job-retraining facilities. You can often find people who need to get practical experience in a new field (you'll often find people learning office skills to reenter the workplace). Again, give them what they need and get what you need.

Finding the help you need to regain the time you are currently giving up is not that hard; you just need to be creative.

One of the biggest reasons you are less productive when you are doing all these small tasks is not just the time you lose—it is the amount of mental energy you are expending thinking about them. The stress and pressure of trying to get something done quickly with other deadlines looming doesn't make you more effective, it makes you less effective at both things, and each ends up taking longer.

GET AGILE TO GET PROFITABLE

When nobody is buying, it is time for you to analyze the problem, get focused, and take action. The faster, more specific action you take, the more successful you'll be. In war, guerrillas often win battles because they are small, agile teams that are organized to get in and have great impact. They succeed where traditional troops don't because they are able to organize quickly, implement quickly, and move to the next target quickly. I want you to adopt that thinking. You are more powerful and more profitable because you can organize, act, implement, and profit more quickly than those around you. It doesn't matter if you are competing for the business against your biggest competitor or a fellow salesperson in your organization. The game goes to the one most focused and fastest to implement.

As you get ready to go to the next chapter, I want you to think fast, be agile, and discover what you can do differently *right now* to leap past your competition. Let's go!

SLUMP BUSTER

AN INTERVIEW WITH SCOTT MARKER

You don't have to work harder. You've got to work harder at working smarter.

— Scott Marker

Scott Marker is an author and professional salesperson. He is also a former mixed martial arts competitor and current referee for mixed martial arts tournaments throughout Idaho. He goes to work every day and sells products for the company that employs him, and he has created a separate business, speaking and writing books. His newest book is called *Let's Get It On! "Real"istic Strategies for Winning the Sales Game.*

> **Dave:** *Scott, what is the big belief that kills salespeople when they are selling during tough times?*
>
> **Scott:** It is that they think that it is all about activity. They think it is about how many calls they make. But that is only half true. You really need to work harder at working smarter. What that means is when the economy is tough and your customers and prospects are cutting

back and they are laying off, their needs change. You have to work smarter to identify the right prospects and decision makers. You can spend a lot of time prospecting people that are nervous about their jobs and who just want to create activity, or you can prospect people who are committed to making a difference at their job, who have the authority to buy. You hear that sales is a numbers game, but it really isn't; it is a game of talking to more of the right people, not just more people. It is a game of what I call *sophisticated basics*. Calling a client on the phone is a basic, but a sophisticated basic is calling on the gatekeeper in advance and telling him that you want to confirm that the person you are sending material to is the right person. Tell him right up front that you don't want to talk to the person right now; it lowers his guard and he is much more likely to give you more information you can use. You say before you hang up, "Oh, by the way, do you currently use *X* product? Who do you get it from?" And then you let him tell you more. Because you aren't asking for the decision maker, he will often tell you a great deal of information you can use to customize the information that you send to the decision maker. And you are developing rapport with the gatekeeper by not trying to get around him. You have to do a lot more up-front work before you get the decision maker on the phone. But that is an elegant, sophisticated use of a basic. You outsell your competitors who believe it is a numbers game—who call, ask for the decision maker, get rejected by the gatekeeper, hang up the phone and dial again. Dialing for dollars doesn't work anymore. You have to be very specific about who you dial and which dollars you are going after.

Dave: *Are relationships more or less important in a tough economy?*

Scott: Relationships are always important, but salespeople need to be very cautious about believing that a relationship or friendship will save a sale today. When the economy is tough and jobs are on the line, people are going to make the decision that they believe will best support keeping their job. They may like you, but if your product isn't making the company money, saving the company money, or doing whatever it is supposed to do, they'll have a hard time defending staying with you based on a relationship alone. My focus has always been to develop the relationship and be a friend but always by being a valued resource as well. Too many salespeople focus on the friend aspect and start to feel entitled. I want to continually add value to the relationship by adding value to the company.

Dave: *Are there shortcuts to selling?*

Scott: Absolutely. You know, I've heard my whole career in martial arts that there are no shortcuts, and that is nonsense, too. The shortcuts come from listening to people who've already made the mistakes and who've developed a better way. You don't have to make all the mistakes I did as a salesperson to be successful; you simply need to find out what my mistakes were and avoid them. You do what worked instead of what didn't. That's why I'm such a huge fan of constant personal development.

Dave: *Do you spend a lot of time looking for new ways of selling by studying more in a tough economy?*

Scott: I don't think I spend more because I *invest* a lot of time, a lot more than my peers, in listening to CDs, reading, and improving my skills. There is a saying in the martial arts that "the more you bleed in the dojo, the less you bleed on the street." What that means to a salesperson is, the more time you invest in training yourself, the more success you'll have when you compete in the marketplace. So I invest as much time as I can in myself. I know that if I can learn just one new technique, get one small idea that modifies something I can do, that I'll have success. The real key to all of that for the sales professional is to implement what you learn. All the learning in the world will do you no good if you just go out and do it your way anyway.

Dave: *What is the best advice you can give sales managers to be sure that their team succeeds over and over again?*

Scott: It applies to both sales managers and salespeople. The answer for sales managers is to teach a sales framework. Teach them exactly what the process is and how it works. In football there may be a lot of variations on plays, but the basics of the game remain the same. You still have to run 100 yards to score a touchdown; you still have four downs; the requirements of the players' position don't change. So when a team is down the coach goes back to the framework and talks about what is happening there and then works on modifications from there. For salespeople it is exactly the same: Learn the framework, learn your position within the team, and rely on your teammates while doing your job to the best of your ability. If you teach and learn the framework of solid selling, you'll have a career that lasts a very long time. I've been a professional salesperson for 20 years and my solid framework serves me very well every day.

Dave: *Final question. Are there more or fewer opportunities in the (2009) economy?*

Scott: For the professional salesperson who wants to work hard and sell, there are more opportunities than ever. People who have the title of salesperson but are really order takers are going to get pushed to the wayside by the professionals. I'm still happy to be a salesperson every day.

2

GET VISIBLE

YOU HAVE TO BE SEEN TO SELL

You can't build relationships with invisible people.
—Dave Lakhani

Most salespeople never spend enough time developing their own personal brand and defining for the customer and their market who *they* are and what *they* stand for. Instead they focus on the company brand and the company image. Don't get me wrong; promoting the company and the company image is important—but being known in your industry makes you more valuable as a resource than a brand alone will. Prospect and customers buy you first; then they buy the idea that you can help them find a solution for their needs, and finally they buy the product.

Ask yourself this question right now: "When someone searches my name in Google, what are the top 10 search results?" Go ahead, type your name in Google right now and see. If the top 10 searches don't include your name and something related to what you sell, if one doesn't include some video of a client who is thrilled with what you did for her, you need look no further to understand why customers are not buying from you. The most credible people can be found in a search. Now search your competitors; do you find them? If not, great, you now have an advantage.

It's time to start being seen so you can sell, so let's get started.

BUILDING YOUR PERSONAL BRAND ONLINE

1. Go to www.godaddy.com right now and buy *yourname* .com. If *yourname*.com is not available, I want you to buy the real*yourname*.com. It is important to have your name in the domain URL because when people search for you we want your domain to come up fast in the search results.

2. Now go to www.weebly.com and set up a free account. You are about to become a Web designer. Don't worry, no technical skills are required; if you can drag and drop and type, you can have a web site up with a blog in about an hour. This is going to become the single most important repository of you on the Web. You'll talk about deals you've closed with which companies (where using company names is allowed). You'll post testimonials about working with you. Don't have testimonials? Don't worry, we'll get to that.

3. Now type this link into your Web browser: www.weebly .com/weebly/main.php. You'll see a page that will show you how to configure your domain (so that when someone types in www.*yourname*.com, your new web site comes up).

It is that simple. You now have a functioning web site where you can begin to build your credibility online. You can make the web site as complicated as you want, but the simpler it is for people to find out what they want to know about you, the better. Here are some things to include on your web site:

- *Your professional bio.* This is a sketch of who you are, your education, your work experience, including past employers, some of your thoughts on the industry you are working in, and a little something personal; if you have a wife or husband and kids, mention them—better yet, put a picture of them with you on the site. If you have hobbies, put some pictures of you doing your hobbies, or at least mention a couple. I like to golf but I'm terrible at it, so in my bio I might write: Avid golfer whose score will make you feel great about your game, no matter how you play! Show them you are real and have a sense of humor.
- *Testimonials.* Create a link on your site called What My Clients Say. On the page that it links to, you'll place quotes from your past clients and videos from current and past clients.
- *Client list.* Create a link to your client list—all the companies you've sold to in the past. This is a place for you to showcase the kind of companies you've sold to so people can see that you have experience selling to companies like theirs. People like buying from people who already have experience with others like them. Your experience is worth a lot, and if they get experience with their relationship with your company, that is a huge plus.
- *Contact Me link.* Create a Contact Me link at the top of your homepage. On your Contact page tell people how they can connect with you. Include your office phone number, your cell number, and your direct e-mail address. (When you write your e-mail address, write it like this: *dave at boldapproach.com*, so that your name and address will not be harvested by spam robots that will fill your inbox with spam.)

- *Your blog.* If you are unfamiliar with blogs and their purpose, let me explain. A blog is like an online diary in which you collect your thoughts about whatever you choose. You don't have to journal the contents of your soul; in fact, I recommend against it. Instead, write about what is going on in your industry. Write about the problems customers have and how they can solve them (using your products and services, where possible). Your blog posts don't have to be long—just long enough to tell your story or make your point. Include a photo where you can; it makes the post more interesting. In your headlines, try to include keywords that your customers might search for, to make it more likely that they'll find your blog in their search.

  For the next 90 days I'd like you to write at least three blog posts per week. If you do and if you follow my instructions about keywords and writing about your industry, you'll be surprised what starts to show up in the searches around your name, your industry, and your products. If you've never read a blog, why not start with mine: http://boldapproach.typepad.com. It will give you an idea of how it works, plus you'll learn many new ideas that I shared in my blog after I wrote this book.

  One last note: No bashing your company, your competitors, or your boss on your blog; leave that to someone else. Your blog is about creating business, not attacking others.

That's it. You've now created your first line of visibility on the Web.

I know what you are thinking; you are thinking, "My company won't let me do that and it seems like a lot of work."

Get over it.

That's right, I said *Get over it.* I have yet to see a company policy that says you can't have a web site about yourself online. The policy may dictate what you can say about the company and your clients, so just follow your company's guidelines. And remember, when you get testimonials, you'll capture two kinds: one about working with you and one about working with your company.

"There he goes again, talking about testimonials," I hear you say. It is much easier than you think to get quality video testimonials. Here's how you do it:

1. You'll need to buy or borrow a digital camera that can capture video. You'll want to get one that does 30 frames per second (fps). I recommend the Canon SD series, which you can find here: http://budurl.com/mycam. This is exactly the camera I use. They cost about $150 as of this writing and they are phenomenal. I've taken mine all over the world and collected testimonials without fail.

2. After you've developed a great relationship with the client and have provided them with an exceptional experience, use this script to ask them for a testimonial: "I hope your experience working with me was phenomenal. *(Pause, they'll most likely say something like, "You were great to work with"; then continue)* Selling is getting more and more competitive, and I'm doing some new things to stay ahead of the curve. I'm wondering if you'd mind saying what you just said into my tiny pocket camera?" *(Pull out the camera and show it to them, then thank my good friend Joel Bauer of www.infotainer.com for that specific camera phrasing, it works wonders.)* Clients will nearly always agree. If they say that their company doesn't allow them to do testimonials, remind them that they are not doing a testimonial about a product or their company; they're simply telling how it was to work with *you*, and that will typically cover the rest.

3. Use the free video-editing software on your PC or Mac to edit the file (it is as easy as drag and drop, cut and

paste), then upload the clip to www.youtube.com. When you upload it be sure to create a title that says, "*<Client name>* leader in *<Industry>* says *<Your name>* is amazing" (or something that they actually did say). In the Tag section put keywords that include your name, the client's name, the client's company name (if you're allowed to use it), your company name (if you can use it), product names, and any other keyword terms potential clients might search on.

You'll be tempted not to take action on the things I just explained in the last few pages, but I'm going to encourage you do these things anyway. The reason nobody's buying from you is not that people don't have money or needs; it is because you are unwilling to break out of your old habits. New ideas create new opportunities. The hidden benefit of having this online presence is that the next time you are looking for a job, you've got one of the most amazing resumes that you can ever send, available right at your fingertips.

Be sure to let people know your web site exists by including your web site link in your signature line in your e-mails and on your business card, and put it anyplace else that you can think of where your clients can learn more about you. Here is what my signature line looks like when you get an e-mail from me:

Dave Lakhani

President, Bold Approach, Inc.

www.boldapproach.com

208-323-2653 - Office

208-279-1254 - Fax

Author of:

Persuasion: The Art of Getting What You Want

Subliminal Persuasion: Influence and Marketing Secrets They Don't Want You to Know

The Power of an Hour: Business and Life Mastery in One Hour a Week

See All My Books Here: http://budurl.com/davesbooks

Read My Blogs:

Subliminal Persuasion

http://www.subliminalpersuasionbook.com/blog

Marketing: The Bold Approach Method

http://boldapproach.typepad.com

See Me Speak

http://budurl.com/seedave

Watch Me on *The Big Idea With Donny Deutsch*

http://budurl.com/bigidea

Follow me here:

http://www.twitter.com/davelakhani

I want people to learn more about me immediately. I want them to dig in and begin building the relationship with me right away. And I want to be sure that I give them enough information for them to develop a bigger picture. I could just as easily direct them to one web site that contained all the information with one link; the choice is yours.

THINK BIGGER: BEING SEEN DOESN'T ALWAYS MEAN IN PERSON

One of the fastest ways to become a resource in your industry is to teach people something that they need to know. Teleseminars and Webinars are two of the best ways to expand your expertise to your clients and prospective customers.

A teleseminar is just what it sounds like—a seminar that is delivered via the phone in a large conference call. You let your prospects know that you'll be teaching them something important in 30–60 minutes and make it worth their while.

For example, let's say that I'm selling point-of-sale (POS) software or hardware solutions in the wine industry. Most of the people who buy POS solutions in that industry are responsible for the winery tasting rooms, which are also retail stores. If I call them or walk in prospecting, they are very unlikely to take my call. If they haven't considered yet whether or not they need a new POS system, they are also unlikely to spend much time talking to me. However, if I give them an opportunity to learn something of value with no expectation of having to buy anything, they become more interested.

So, what I would do is line up an interview with Gary V. of www.winelibrary.tv and ask him if I could interview him for a program I'm doing for my clients. I'd choose Gary because I know he is aggressive about spreading his message and he has high credibility in the wine industry. The first thing I'd talk to him about is profitability in his tasting room and how he made the decision to focus online and where the profitability was there. Then I'd ask him about how he used technology to increase profitability in his tasting room and what areas were most important to him. I'd ask *him* if the best benefits of my POS product would serve him. Now, at this point I don't care if he already has a system in place—I only want to hear him say how important that feature and the resultant benefit are.

The result would be a 30- to 60-minute interview with Gary that I'll have recorded and that everyone can dial in and listen to and even ask a few questions at the end. It is a win for both of us—Gary gets to further expose winelibrary.tv and gets to connect with real fans, and I get a teaching tool I can use again and again to incent prospects. Reusing content like this is the most effective way to get the most from it. I'll put it on a CD and send it to prospects or give it to them as a gift for seeing me. I'd also make it available on my personal web site, to reinforce the value of what I can do and what I bring to the table.

There is a powerful sales lesson here, too: Using this kind of tool allows you to build trust and credibility in advance. It demonstrates that you are connected and that you are working with people of the highest caliber. It has a very subliminal effect on the person with whom you are interacting.

RESOURCES

Get a free conference bridge that will hold a minimum of 96 people at one of these two places; both give you recording functionality through the phone:

- www.freeconferencecall.com
- www.conferencetown.com

For Webinar service go to www.gotowebinar.com, a paid service that allows you to record both voice and video for replay.
If you want to automate the reproduction and shipping of your CD, I recommend using www.kunaki.com. Or you can always simply copy, print, label, and ship them yourself using inkjet or laser labels available from an office supply store.

Being seen to sell doesn't necessarily mean that you need to spend more time face to face with your customer (though that is often a good choice); it means that you need to spend more time being visible. Your potential clients will buy from the person they see as the most visible and whom they see as having the most expertise in any given market.

DEVELOP YOUR PERSONA

Pretty people make more money than ugly people. Skinny people make more money than fat people. Tall people make more money than short people. Now, you can argue with me all you want, but it won't change the fact that most humans have a built-in set of prejudices that they apply in any given situation. They are more likely to hire or give a raise to the taller person; it is a predictable pattern. I teach a program around the patterns of predictable people,™ and in the program we talk about what causes or cues people to make a certain decision or to say yes to your proposition. The single best way to get the yes is to show up as the person that they expect or desire to do business with. Well-spoken, well-dressed salespeople instill a sense of confidence without saying a word. When people see you, they judge you before you speak, and when listening to you on the phone, they judge you by the quality of your voice and words. If you want to sell more when sales are difficult, focus on showing up as the person your client expects.

DRESS TO LEAD

Most salespeople dress far too casually or haphazardly to fully meet the expectation of their audience. They feel that business casual is good enough, and it simply isn't. When I'm dressed better than my peers, better than my competition, and when I do it consistently, I stand out in a crowd. I look like the leader, and your clients want to buy from people who meet their expectation of trust. When you see CEOs on television and when you meet them in person, they are wearing the uniform of a CEO—a suit. Uniforms cause an unconscious response in us. We've been conditioned to respond in a certain way to each kind of uniform; a suit gets a completely different reaction than jeans and a polo shirt. Set yourself up to succeed, dress better, and you'll sell more. Oh, and while you're at it, upgrade your accessories—get a very nice high-quality pen to write with, something that makes an impact and makes you feel good writing with it. Buy a Moleskine notebook (Google it) to keep notes in, or get a very nice leather legal pad holder or attaché.

All these rules apply equally to men or women. Look the part and get the sale.

SPEAK TO THEIR LISTENING

Improve your voice and your vocabulary and you'll increase your sales as well. Well-spoken people appear more intelligent than those who are not well spoken. You don't need to use a whole dictionary of 50-dollar words, but you do need a vocabulary that gives you the ability to use language that is precise and clear. Spend five minutes a day learning a new word of the day and watch what happens to your income in the coming year. Subscribe to the free word of the day e-mail at www .dictionary.com. The best way to integrate the new word into your vocabulary is to say it out loud several times, then use it in a sentence, write it down in a sentence, and finally, commit to using it at least 10 times in your conversation during the day. Also, write it down on a Post-it note and put it somewhere you can see it the rest of the day. Then, before you go to sleep, repeat the word 10 more times and say it in five different sentences before drifting off. You'll find yourself experiencing tremendous recall and a rapid increase in your vocabulary.

SAY WHAT THEY WANT TO HEAR

Learning how to speak, how to use your voice without a lot of filler words, and improving the quality of your voice will also enhance trust and improve people's experience with you on the phone. If you'll just spend a few moments with a voice-coaching CD each week for 90 days, you'll be amazed at what you can do with your voice and how it changes how people react to you. You can create instant confidence with your voice. Dr. Carol Fleming has the best, fastest, easiest-to-use program I've seen and it is only $21; grab it today and see for yourself what happens. You can find the CD here: http://budurl.com/myvoice.

I can't tell you how many times I get called back because people want to tell me that I have a voice for radio or they want to know if I do radio. My voice only sounds that way because I invested the time necessary to make me stand out from my peers. I'm in my forties now and I still invest in my wardrobe, my vocabulary, and my voice, and I've been the top salesperson in every organization I've ever sold in. You will be, too. Before you get started, I've heard all the arguments about how to dress, about "wasting time" on things like voice training. And I'm going to tell you something: You are reading this book because you want an incremental edge, you want something that will help you when everyone is struggling. This book is a tool kit and these are your tools. I promise you one thing for sure—these tools won't work if you don't try them. And by the way, all this information is based on sound psychological research. I'll always choose to give myself the edge and appeal to people's unconscious expectations. You have to choose: Do you want more of what you've been getting, or do you want more sales?

GET FACE TO FACE

Prospects and clients like to put a face to a name. They also like to see you so that the communication feels more complete. There are two fast tools that I use to get face to face with clients who are distant. The first is Skype (www.skype.com). Skype is an Internet-based phone and videoconferencing system that allows you to have a two way video conversation with your prospect or client. Just like dialing a phone, you call the client, enable video, and have a conversation—except that you are able to see each other and engage the visual aspect of communication missing over the phone alone. There is great persuasive value in leveraging two-way video communication because it encourages trust by allowing people to take in the nonverbal portion of the communication that is typically missing when you are not face to face.

The next technique to give that personal feel and to increase your personal brand equity is to use prerecorded video. If you have or are using the video camera I spoke of earlier, it is very easy to create video on the fly, but any digital video camera will work. You simply fire up your camera wherever you are, make sure you have a good light source and clutter-free background, and then start filming yourself speaking to your client or prospect. The purpose of the video is to create a very succinct, to-the-point video that deeply engages the viewer. Make the message personal and memorable. Video messages break through the clutter because people still don't use them very often. Video messages also improve your brand identity; people begin to associate you as being different and memorable.

But that's not all—customers want to develop relationships with people they trust, have confidence in, and like. It is your responsibility to properly develop that trust with your customers.

POSITIONING PLUS PACKAGING EQUALS DESIRE— AND A DESIRE IS A BUYER

You already know that people don't buy what they need, they buy what they want. All purchase decisions are based on meeting the emotional needs of the person making the decision. To be successful in tough times, it is necessary to differentiate yourself and your offering from those of the competition. The best way to do that is to first identify the prospect's real need. If you are selling automobiles and believe you are in the transportation business, then any old vehicle will do. If, on the other hand, you realize that your single biggest job as a salesperson is to identify and amplify the *desire* of a customer, you'll look deeper. You'll realize that transportation is a very base expectation. In reality, a car is more than that; a car represents freedom and independence, it represents status, and it often represents an extension of the identity of the person driving it. People buying cars are looking for people to sell them cars that enhance their freedom and independence, their status, or their identity. Knowing what your clients want and what desire they are fulfilling allows you to present perfect and irresistible choices.

You enhance desire by allowing people to experience as many of the results of having your product or service in advance as you can. In the example of the car, if you know that freedom and independence is what people want from the car, you may arrange for them to drive the car overnight, giving them the ability to really have an experience. Then the next morning, you show up and offer to take their freedom and independence away . . . or fill out the paperwork to extend it. No one wants to lose what they desire.

MAKE YOUR EXPERTISE KNOWN

The most effective way to create new sales is to create desire and trust. Developing and demonstrating your expertise allows you to position yourself ahead of your competitors. There are many ways you can demonstrate your expertise to your clients and prospects and leverage your expert status to develop new leads. Let's look at a few of the highest-value, highest-visibility tactics.

- *Write articles and distribute them online.* Writing articles demonstrates your knowledge of your industry, product, or service. Start out by writing 1000-word articles and post them online at www.ezine.com as well as submitting them to your industry trade journals and to your trade journal's blogs. Published articles give you strong credibility and increase lead flow.
- *Create white papers.* Like articles, white papers give you expert status and increase visibility. Distribute them on your company web site, through industry organizations, and directly to your prospects and customers. Pick a

significant problem they have for which you can provide the best solution and create your first white paper.

- *Get nominated.* Get nominated for an American Business Award. Go to www.stevieawards.com and nominate yourself for an American Business Award in the category of Sales Executive of the Year. You could very well win, and even if you don't you can forever say you were nominated for an American Business Award for Sales Executive of the Year. Be sure you put your nomination in all your correspondence. Search for other industry awards to which you can submit your name and your products. The only way to win awards is to fill out the forms and submit them; you've got everything to gain by trying. Or, as Hunter S. Thompson used to say, "Buy the ticket, take the ride."

- *Blog.* Remember that web site with a blog that you built (you did build it ... right)? Start creating blog posts around your areas of expertise. When you talk to clients about things you've written about, be sure to direct them to your blog so that they can read more about you and experience your expertise more deeply.

Building your personal brand, developing your expertise, and telling the world about both takes some effort on your part, but the payoff is tremendous. This is a short-term effort that will lead to very long-term gain and allow you to write your ticket no matter where you are. I know that some of these ideas are unconventional, and they are supposed to be. Do one *different* thing today and see what happens.

People want someone to care about, an idea they can care about; they want those things from someone they can believe in. You have to be visible to sell all that. You have to focus on being the best in the world at what you do and letting people know about it. No one wants to buy from the third best person in the industry.

3

GET CONNECTED

HOW TO FIND BUYERS WHO ARE
READY TO BUY NOW

*"What else can I sell when nobody is buying?" is the wrong
question. The right question is, "How do I connect with the
people who are buying what I'm already selling?"*
—Dave Lakhani

I have several thousand followers on Twitter.com, a platform
we'll talk about more later in this chapter. I posed this question
to those people: "What is your toughest sales question about
selling when nobody is buying?" The one question that got
asked over and over again was some version of this: "How can
we determine what people *are* still spending money on?" And
that is exactly the wrong question. The answer is: You don't
sell when nobody's buying by flitting from product to product,
service to service, looking for the easy sale. You focus. The right
question to ask is, "Who is still spending money on what I sell,
and how do I connect with them?" That question will break any
slump and get you back on track.

The question that my followers on Twitter asked is a very
common response to sales slumps. Salespeople often assume

that they need to find a new product to sell—that people have simply quit buying their products and must be buying something else. Typically what really happens in changing industries and economies is that sales cycles extend. More focus is put on every step of the cycle and the sale itself is more strongly scrutinized to see if it is in fact still justified. But when you ask yourself the question, "Who is still buying what I'm selling and how do I connect with them?" you begin digging deeper.

Through the rest of this chapter I'm going to show you how to get connected with everyone who is or could be buying your product. You'll learn how to use the most current tools online right now and the strategies to make them work. If you aren't already familiar with the term *social media,* you've likely at least heard it. *Social media* relates to the emerging media online that are not controlled by large media corporations but are generated by average people like you and me. It also incorporates social networking sites such as Facebook and microblogging platforms such as Twitter. In the extended learning section of this book, contained in the Appendix, I've asked Dr. Rachna Jain, one of the nation's top experts on social media and the psychology of social media, to create a very powerful introduction to the topic, including a social media plan that you can initiate quickly and easily.

THE NEW PROSPECTING TOOLS YOU AREN'T USING TO MAXIMIZE SALES

The Internet has provided salespeople with a virtual treasure trove of tools to find new prospects. It also provides you with more information than you have likely ever had on a prospect—their needs and motivations as well as how to reach out and touch them.

GOOGLE ALERTS

Google Alerts (www.google.com/alerts) is the first of your online intelligence tools for effective prospecting. Google Alerts does the job of automating your search for information. When you set up a Google alert for a keyword, phrase, or name, Google sets about searching and immediately notifying you when it finds new information about your name or search term. You get an e-mail immediately showing what information was found and a link directly to it, including that information that is currently in the news that day.

Let's say that I sell a service that stages, deploys, and installs point-of-sale (POS) solutions for chain retailers. Now, I could call every chain retailer and go through the process of trying to reach the chief technology officer to ask him about whether or not the company is planning to roll out a system or whether they are considering a new system in the next year that would require technical services help. *Or* I could just set up a series of Google Alerts. I'm going to use Macy's in my example. Here are the alerts I might set up to get all the information I can on each company that I want to track:

"Macy's point of sale." I want to know what Macy's is doing with its point of sale, so I include all the words within quotations because I want an exact match. If I just put "point of sale" in quotes and left Macy's outside the quotes I'd get every reference with the term "point of sale" and the word Macy's, but when I put the whole thing in quotes I only get references to Macy's point-of-sale activities.

"Macy's CIO." I want to know what Macy's chief information officer is talking about publicly. This gives me information I can use to build a relationship, or it could alert me to new opportunities.

"<Name of> Macy's CIO." I want to know what he or she is talking about as well. This will give me ideas about what is important to that CIO.

"Macy's rolls out technology." I want to know whenever Macy's is rolling out technology—in fact, I'd set up another alert

that is a generic "technology rollout" so that I can see every-one who is announcing technology rollouts, to see if there is business that I should be pursuing.

"Replacing point of sale." I'd use this alert to see anyone who was replacing their PoS system, including Macy's.

"Technology overhaul" Macy's. I'd use this alert to see all technology overhauls, plus Macy's in particular.

The list could go on and on, but you get the idea. You want to cover as many of the possible terms that could alert you to new business or that could allow you to better determine who is involved in projects that are ongoing and how you might contact them.

When I train sales teams about how to use Google Alerts, I teach them to think about using them to collect the following information:

- Changes in status of projects or announcements of upcoming projects
- Names of people and intelligence on people involved in projects
- Financial information about the company that lets me understand its position
- Information I can use to start a conversation or move it forward
- My competitors' names and business names and my prospects' names and business names so that if my competitors start talking publicly about what they are doing or working on, I find out about it as soon as possible. I've often swooped in on some business when one of my competitors mentions online somewhere that they are working on a project. They did the work of prospecting for me, and their loose lips online gave me the hot lead.

By setting up the alerts, I automate a lot of the research that I'd normally have to do and let Google do the work for me. You'll be consistently amazed at the opportunities you find and at the information you collect using this strategy. Furthermore, to build on a strategy for building your reputation and expert status, as we talked about in the last chapter, you can use Google Alerts to direct you to blogs, forums, and other places where you can comment and link back to your blog or company web site. Commenting on blogs and in forums is a great way to continue to widen your web of influence.

LEVERAGE YOUR LINKS ON LINKEDIN.COM

LinkedIn.com is a powerful networking tool that allows you to maintain contact with people in your network and expand your reach through your network. One of the things that makes LinkedIn so powerful is the levels that you must go through to connect with other people on the network. You aren't just able to browse and add contacts; you must have a connection to these people and they must accept your contact. Once they've accepted you, you can see the people in their network as well, and if you are not connected to someone in their network you can use a series of tools to get the introduction. If you want to see an example of how LinkedIn works, visit my profile at http://budurl.com/davel (and since you are a reader of my book, add yourself as a contact—you are now part of my network).

The larger your network grows with people who legitimately connect with you, the shorter the line to a connection with someone you'd like to meet. Here are some of the most profitable connections on LinkedIn.com:

- Co-workers current and past
- Clients current and past

- Those in your physical network
- Business partners
- Vendors
- High school, college, military, social organization, and fraternal colleagues
- Board members of any boards on which you sit

Again, the idea of creating as wide a network as you can is to reach out to and through that network to the people you want to meet and connect with. Here are a couple of the most powerful strategies you can use immediately; then you can experiment more with the tool and learn what is possible. Start by searching for people you know from the categories in the preceding list and send them an e-mail asking to connect with you on Linkedin.com. Build the number of direct connections as fast as you can, because that is what will begin to give you connections to others that you can leverage.

Let's do a simple search and see how many prospects are available for a topic. I'm going to use the title VP of Sales as my search for this example because those people can typically hire me. Go to LinkedIn.com, sign in (set up an account if you haven't already; it's free). At the top right of the page you'll see a search box and search button. Just to the right of the search button you'll see a link that says Advanced Search. Click the Advanced Search button. I'm going to fill in the box next to Title with *VP of Sales*. Next I'll choose industries in the check box section to the right of the title box. I'm choosing Financial Services, Insurance, and Pharmaceuticals. When I click the Search button, the search returns 7041 potential prospects with whom I could connect and call on to sell my books or sales training.

The first three pages of people on the results page I'm either already connected with; that is over 30 people I'm directly connected to or one connection away from. Here is what is great: Anyone that I'm one or two connections away from presents dozens more opportunities. All I need to do is choose the Get Introduced button next to the person's name I'd like to connect with and fill in the form. When I click Send, the site will send an e-mail asking the person I'm connected to, who is also connected to the person I want to meet, an e-mail asking that person to introduce the two of us. This is what makes this site so powerful: I'm getting an introduction to a contact from someone that contact knows, so my chances of success in connecting go up exponentially.

Using the advanced search function I can search for prospects by:

- Industry
- Name
- Company
- Keyword, including product names and so on

You are limited only by your ability to search in terms of the potential prospects you can connect with.

The next question to ask is, "How do I want people to find me?" When you set up your profile it is important that you include information that is clear about what you currently do, so people who are searching can find you when they are looking for connections in a specific area. I just did a search for tour guides in New York City and 300+ people came up in the search results, several of whom I am connected to already because their profiles included information about being a tour guide. When you fill out your profile, pay particular attention to the headline; it is one of the most important pieces of the puzzle. Be sure you say something that appeals to the people who might be searching for you, your industry, or your products or services.

There are many more powerful features on LinkedIn that you'll discover as you explore, but the last that I want to talk about is the "Ask a Question" function. Under the Answers tab at the top of the page you'll find a link that reads Ask a Question. You can ask a question that will go out to the LinkedIn network and to up to 200 of your connections. This is a powerful way to do product or service research, to get specific information about an industry, and much more. However, you should not ask for people who can connect you to other people; that is what your network is for. But you could ask for help on a strategy to reach someone that was tough to reach—say, the President or Warren Buffett.

Building an online network will give you not only new opportunities but a look at what is going on in a number of different industries. If you ever decide to change jobs or want to explore your career options, you've also now got a network to go out to, giving you an edge over many job seekers.

TWITTER YOUR WAY TO NEW SALES NOW

Twitter is the up-and-coming online communications platform. If you haven't experienced Twitter yet, it is technically referred to as a *microblogging* platform. Twitter allows you to say anything you want in 140 characters. You type into the message box, press Send, and everyone who follows you is able to see what you have to say. In return, you are able to follow what your followers are talking about, too. What is interesting and useful about Twitter is how quickly new information is passed around. In many cases, breaking news is reported by firsthand viewers on Twitter.

The power of Twitter for salespeople is twofold. First, you are able to keep tabs on many people at once and see what they are talking about, so you get a feel for many things about them. Second, and probably the most important, is the ability Twitter gives you to reach out and get detailed information quickly.

While I was writing this book I sent this tweet (a *tweet* is a Twitter entry) to my list of followers: "If you are in sales, how do you use Twitter to your advantage?" Within 30 seconds I had these responses:

@davidbeking: @davelakhani use http://search.twitter.com and find prospects! you can search keywords and "industry jargon" to connect with prospects!

@DrWright1: I use it to target skin care prospects for product placement on www.wrightplacetv.com because they understand product placement.

lynettepatter: @davelakhani I use twitter to 1.Promote my biz 2.Spread health info 3.Connect with my clients & see how their day is going

Try it right now—go to Twitter.com, go to the search link, and type in some industry jargon and see what comes up and while you are there. Follow those people who are in your industry and who are talking about your industry. Then when you are done, try this tool: www.monitter.com, where you can type in industry keywords and phrases and watch conversations happening in real time. Join in the conversations that are most appropriate to you and your business. Don't just jump in and say you have something to sell; ask questions, provide information, give opinions, and share resources. Do what you'd do if a friend were discussing the same subject with you; you wouldn't try to hard-sell them, you'd share information and resources, so do the same on Twitter.

The key to successful Twittering is to keep the conversation moving forward. And be sure that when you see people discussing your industry or your products (or competitive products), you follow those people; they are your audience. And your audience will grow because typically people will follow you in turn when you add to the conversation. There are many examples of companies that use Twitter very effectively: The Home Depot (http://twitter.com/thehomedepot), Popeye's

Chicken (http://twitter.com/popeyeschicken), and Comcast (http://twitter.com/comcastcares), to name a few. Take a look at their pages and see how they use Twitter to extend their brands and create sales.

Another tool that will allow you to stand out using twitter is Twitpic (www.twitpic.com). Twitpic allows you to take a picture on your cell phone and e-mail it to your account, where it is stored, and then sends it out on Twitter for you. I often use this technology to show new products, ideas, or people I meet at trade shows and industry or networking events. When I'm traveling I'll also include photos of interesting places or things that I see, to add some texture to my conversations and keep them interesting. The key is that it is fast and it keeps the conversation interesting and engaging.

There are a couple of tips that make searching and tweeting easier. Often when topics are trending, people will but the hashtag (#) in front of a word—for example, if you are doing a Twitter search for a program I did called "Renegades of Persuasion" and you go to the search box and put in #ROP, you'll get all the tweets related to that event in the returned search. The same is true of companies—just try it: Type in some of your favorite companies, such as #Starbucks, #Macy's, #Pizza Hut, or any other, and see what people are talking about. You can also do this with your competitors and competitive products; this technique gives you great information you can use to sell with. You'll often find trends about product issues or the like on Twitter long before you'll hear about them elsewhere.

Be sure to include the # hashtag when you are tweeting about something specific. If you are at a trade show, for example, put the hashtag in front of the name of the event, or if you are talking about a product or even a city, put the hashtag before it. Others who are interested in the topic will then be able to find you and connect with you.

Comment on other people's tweets and "retweet" relevant ones by including *rt + <their twitter name> + <the message>*. A good retweet would look like this:

RT: Just started following @billwillardjr very interesting guy, follow him.

The best way to comment on a tweet is to simply respond to it with your thoughts.

When you are sending links to your web site or any other site, rather than send really long URLs that often break, use a link-shortening tool such as www.tinyurl.com or www.budurl.com. I like Budurl.com; for $4 a month you can get stats to see how often people are following your links on Twitter or anyplace else you choose to use them. For example, you've seen me use Budurl.com throughout this book to make it easy for you to find places online that I'm talking about. You can also add your own extensions of between 4 and 20 characters to the link you want to shorten so it looks like budurl.com/IChoose, or whatever you choose.

For many of you reading this book, you are going to say that these things take too much time or that they are for nerds only; real business people don't have time for this online stuff. And you'll be wrong on both accounts. The world of prospecting and connecting with customers is changing, and you have to change with it if you plan on making your quota next month. A lot of people will say that their prospects are not on Twitter nor are they using social media. Reality is that many of them may be on Twitter and using it for something else or just learning it, which gives you a unique opportunity to connect. I know there are still a lot of people who walk around neighborhoods selling vacuum cleaners door to door, but that isn't the most efficient way of selling them anymore. The way you've been prospecting and selling may be greatly enhanced by adding tools such as Twitter. Don't be a doubter—be an implementer and see what happens.

SOCIAL MEDIA IS A SMALL TOWN

If you think of the Internet and social media as you would about living in a small town, you'll see how quickly and closely people are connected. It is not just important, it's imperative that you understand how these tools work if you hope to remain competitive long term. The deeper your network and the wider your web of influence, the faster you will get more sales. The Internet makes the world very small very quickly.

When you think of social media as a small town, it helps you comport yourself in a way that is appropriate and helpful while still being able to do your job. Don't do or say anything online that you wouldn't do or say in public in your hometown.

TRADITIONAL NETWORKING AND CONNECTING

I'd be remiss if I didn't talk to you about what you are doing to connect with people in person. Even though attendance is down greatly today, you still need to go to trade shows, mixers, Chamber of Commerce meetings, and the like, but you need a different strategy. You've probably rightly identified that decision makers often don't show up at those events—but influencers do. As you create a strategy to sell more, you need to cast a wider web of influence so that you create more opportunities to connect.

As you begin to explore and exploit the online tools available to you, you'll begin to see things like meetups and tweet-ups and other meetings of people moving their relationships from online to offline. In the game of sales, the best-connected people win again and again. You must invest time in face-to-face connections as well as online ones. But here's how to do it right.

Invest your time in very specific interest groups. If you know that decision makers don't show up at the mixers and Chamber of Commerce after-hours events and you don't want to go to those, then don't go. Invest your time by going to very specific vertical events. So, rather than the Chamber mixer, you could go to the building and zoning fact-finding session. You show up where the decision makers are, or at least where the deep influencers are. You spend your time influencing them.

There are two exceptions to this rule. The first is if you can host an event. If you or your company is the host, you show up no matter what. Hosting an event gives you extra credibility. It also gives you a reason to personally call the CEO or other high-level executives in the companies that are invited, to personally invite them to the event. And if you are going to host the event, be sure to have a tour or schedule private meetings with key players and decision makers at the event. It is important to be a gracious host, but don't forget what you are there to do.

The second exception is if you can position yourself as an expert or an authority and speak at networking groups. Speaking in front of a group of your peers and prospects as an expert is a powerful means of developing new leads quickly. Many of your competitors will not take this route; it makes them uncomfortable and they are unprepared. Plan in advance for these opportunities and then pitch the idea to the groups. Here is a dirty little secret: I've been on the committees of many of these events, not to mention a speaker at scores of them now, and they virtually all need leads or good people who can share valuable information. Be their go-to guy. The more you are on stage, the more you educate, the more people talk about you and you get to control the conversation. Top-of-mind awareness is about conversation domination, and your goal is to always be in the conversations that potential customers are having, whenever they have them.

INTEGRATED INFLUENCE

Never forget the value of face-to-face connections, and never underestimate the power of the new prospecting tools that you've just learned about. Furthermore, know that new tools will always be emerging. Part of your job is to stay on top of the new places your prospects gather and insert yourself into the conversation.

In an earlier chapter I talked about the need to be seen in order to sell, and connecting is the "doing" part of being seen. I look forward to seeing you on Twitter and Facebook and LinkedIn. If you haven't already connected with me on those sites or are not rushing there to do it this moment, rest assured that your competition is, and you are getting farther behind. See you on the other side.

Oh, one more reason to follow me? That is where I give all kinds of cool, free bonuses to my readers and followers, such as books, CDs, and DVD sets. But hey, the choice is yours—you can do what you've always done and get the same results, or you can get busy and get connected with me and your prospects and win the new game of sales so that you never have to worry about who isn't buying.

RESOURCES

www.tweetdeck.com

www.seesmic.com

Use either service to more efficiently manage your Twitter account.

www.nearbytweets.com

Use this site to find others near your address.

http://twtQpon.com

Use this site to create Twitter coupons.

4

GET DIGITAL AND GET OFF THE ROAD

SELL TO BUYERS AT THEIR DESKS FROM YOURS

The proper use of technology explodes territories and opportunities, yet most companies and most salespeople still don't use it consistently.

—Dave Lakhani

When the economy is bad or sales are slumping, among the first things that get highly scrutinized and often reduced are travel expenses. Frankly, that could be the best thing that ever happens to you. If you are not currently fully exploiting today's technology, you are leaving money and sales on the table every day. Technology explodes territories and opportunities by putting your presentation in front of the client immediately. If they have 15 minutes to talk, a multimedia web-based conversation with you is quite often much more effective than a trip for a fact-finding meeting to see if you are a good fit for each other. It also makes you much more productive and saves a tremendous amount of time. There is also the added benefit of just driving prospects to a web site where you lead them through the presentation, and they have the opportunity to go back through it again and again or to pull out specific information they can use.

When industries or economies change, downsizing often takes place, quickly leaving more work for fewer people. Buyers are much more selective in choosing vendors and often stick with current vendors because the time investment in seeing new potential vendors seems too high.

In 2008, when President (then candidate) Barak Obama was making his big campaign push, we saw politics start to change in Washington. Many suggest that Obama was successful due to his use of technology and social media to reach people where they lived. If it works for the President of the United States, it will work for you as well. Here I'm going to show you several ways of leveraging selling technologies to your benefit, and we'll build on some we've already spoken about.

A CROWD OF ONE OR MANY, RIGHT
AT YOUR COMPUTER

While I was researching this book I spoke to literally dozens of salespeople and sales trainers about how they were leveraging desktop technology in order to sell to their clients. The answer was that they were not. Many were using a CRM solution, but only a very small number did remote presentations or Webinars to their prospects or clients. Those who were familiar with the technology often said that someone else did the presenting and it was more technical in nature—for example, showing a software application.

Here's the real rub: Virtually everyone I talked to said that they spend a lot of time putting together presentations and that they spend even more time (including lost family time) and expense getting to a client's office and presenting, only to get a no. Or they got all the information they needed, put together a proposal, sent if off, and never heard from anyone again, or the client rejected the proposal out of hand with no questions.

Whenever this happens, sales managers are quick to tell salespeople to get more proposals in front of prospects because "it's a numbers game." It isn't really a numbers game when you are playing and losing at that level; it is a game of not being heard or not having the opportunity to gather information and develop a response. The end result is a lot of time and a lot of effort, often wasted.

Over the past five years I've spoken to C-level executives and buyers around the world as I've trained their sales teams to overcome their reluctance to meet with salespeople—and overwhelmingly I get one of two answers. The first is that the salesperson didn't inspire confidence that he had the right solution; the second was that they were worried about wasting time with unqualified vendors. Trained buyers also report that they routinely reject approaches so that they create pressure on salespeople, causing them to give in more easily to price demands when they do finally accept the meeting. Webinars and online presentation-sharing solutions take those objections away immediately.

Here's why Webinars and online presentations work: Your sales and success at prospecting go up and down because you don't present the very best material the same way each time. When you work from memory, you leave little pieces out, you forget the order of things, and you give a different presentation, though it seems the same each time. But when you deliver your most powerful material in the way that you know tends to get more conversions, you get—you guessed it—more conversions. The key is to present your material consistently each time.

Using PowerPoint allows you to present the same way each time. It also gives you the flexibility to answer any questions that may come up and move people back to the process. Moving away from the process and following tangents without coming back also impacts your ability to predictably close.

Here's how it works: If you typically need to be face to face to do your first pitch (after you've gotten the yes to see you), this process will allow you to do the same presentation from your desk. The first step is to create your pitch. When I'm selling and I want to get to an appointment or the next step in my process, I understand two things going in. The first is that the better I educate my prospect, the more likely they are to say yes to what comes next, quickly opt out, or allow me to disqualify them. The second thing I know is that the more interactive time people spend with me up front, the more likely they are to convert. There is a direct correlation between investment of effort, emotion, and action-taking behavior. The more actions people agree to take with me, the more likely they are to go through the complete process and close at the end.

Creating your pitch will be very straightforward; you are simply going to outline your most powerful proposition, the one that always works with qualified prospects to get them to say yes. You then break that up into PowerPoint slides that contain one big idea and one powerful graphic per slide. Now, that big idea is there for the prospect to grab hold of and allows you to talk as much as you need to about it. The graphic should tie in closely to the big idea. If you are talking about differences in your product versus others, show yours and theirs. Use arrows that fly in to point out the differences, and put Xs over the competitive product to show what it is missing. This kind of interactivity causes people to become more engaged and to remember the differentiation.

This process is nearly equivalent to sitting in front of prospects and showing them the differences in person. If you want to show them how something works or demonstrate the product in action (which is a very powerful technique), create a video and include it. You can load it up on YouTube.com or Viddler.com and simply ask the prospect to type the link into their browser and watch the movie. Try to make the movie no longer than one or two minutes, if possible. Go for big key points rather than trying to show every move, unless you can show everything in that amount of time. Create enough slides that you can use about one slide per minute of time that you'd normally spend asking for the next step. The reason for one slide per minute is that you want to keep prospects' attention, keep them focused on what is happening on the screen. If you take more than a minute, you begin to lose their attention. Don't know how many minutes you need? Then you need to role-play this with someone on your team or simply time your next presentation.

Remember, the idea here is to be able to more deeply educate the people with whom you are interacting and to condition them to the use of technology so that you can do more without leaving your desk and offer multiple ways of experiencing what you have to offer.

Some things to keep in mind when you build your presentation: Keep the effects in the slides to a minimum. Don't try to do too much, because it often translates to slow or jerky viewing on the other end. They need to play video locally on their end or they are not going to get the sound, so it is a good idea to tell them to open another browser and type in the URL you give them to see the video and then have them close the browser so that they go back to your presentation.

One company that uses this selling process very effectively is www.LandBankNation.com. When you engage with them, their only goal is to get you to sit through an online presentation. LandBankNation.com's CEO, Darren Proulx, knows that engaged interest equals buyers, so the company makes sure that they have you engaged, and when they then meet with people in person they are much more comfortable and familiar. Those people are also more likely to commit because they made two investments of time.

Here are the items that you should include in every presentation:

- A picture of you so that prospects know who they are talking to; faces increase responsiveness and make you real.
- A picture of the product or the result people get from using your product or service.
- Testimonials with graphics (a picture of the person) or video (preferable) that allow people to see that they are not the first person to do use your product or service and demonstrate what they can expect to experience. The psychological law of transference of power and credibility makes this incredibly powerful. Dr. Robert Cialdini has done a tremendous amount of research around this idea and the idea of social proof; all the studies demonstrate how much more effective this element makes your persuasive efforts.

Here is an example of how my script goes when I have a prospect on the phone. I use this now when I'm selling consulting services, and I've developed versions of it for many of my clients, who use it very successfully. Typically, when you are at the qualifying stage, you can lead clients to a place where they ask you to tell them more; this is where they are making their decisions about whether or not to invest in spending time with you.

Prospect: Tell me more about your product or service. We use Supplier X; how do you compare?

Me: Thanks for asking. I'd like to answer that question specifically, may I? *(This is a traditional "yes set" answer and* *it also forces the yes, because how else would they want you to answer it?)*

Prospect: Yes.

Me: Perfect. Are you in front of your computer right now? Good. Please type the following address into your browser. *(Give them an address that you've shortened using* budurl.com; *you'll have a good idea if they are looking by watching your stats online.)* I want to walk you very quickly through the answer to your question; this is the fastest, most effective way to give you the information you require. It typically takes about 15 seconds to load. Just let me know when you can see my screen on your PC.

Prospect: Okay, it's on the screen.

Me: Great, this is working very well. I've found that this is a much quicker way of answering your questions rather than trying to give you a bunch of bullet points verbally, and I want to be respectful of your time. It works better to just show you as we talk. And as you can see on your screen now . . . *(Then you launch right into your presentation.)*

This is a very tightly tested script, and fewer than 2 percent of the people who listen to it say no. When they do say no, it is usually because they are not in front of a PC, and for that other small percentage who just don't want to do it, that is fine. Simply continue your presentation in the traditional format and go for the face-to-face meeting or whatever you would have done in the past.

There are a number of software selections that you can make to do a Webinar. Both solutions I'm about to mention allow you to host multiple people so that you can easily do group presentations. One of the values of Webinars is that you can sell to multiple people at the same time. WebEx (www.WebEx .com) is by far the best known in the corporate environment. The other up-and-comer that has a lot of merit that I use is called GoToWebinar (www.GoToWebinar.com). Both pieces of software are very intuitive and easy to use, and their learning curve is very short.

HOW TO PRESENT TO PROSPECTS 24 HOURS A DAY USING WEBINARS

One of the great things about Webinars is that they can be recorded and replayed any time. The best way to present to an audience who is passively but proactively searching out your product is to record your Webinar as you deliver it using a program such as www.camtasia.com and then include a link in the signature line of your e-mail and in any other places where it is appropriate.

There is great value in taking this approach, because it allows you to heighten desire and interest in a nonthreatening way. Furthermore, walking people through the same presentation in person has the psychological effect of making them feel like they are hearing something that they are familiar with, and familiarity breeds comfort and increases the likelihood of buying behavior.

MASS PROSPECTING

In an earlier chapter I talked to you about using teleseminars to create expert status in your existing prospects and clients. Teleseminars are also a very powerful way to prospect large groups at once. The technology that's available allows you to easily host 100–200 people on a conference call all at once, where you can take them through your sales pitch.

Your focus in a teleseminar is the same whether you're selling products or services: You want to qualify, intensify desire and trust, provide proof that your solution is the best one for people like them, and then move them to the next step in your process.

Depending on the complexity of your product or service, try to produce events that last under an hour. People have a limited amount of time and limited attention spans. The longer your event goes, the higher the likelihood that they will become distracted, multitask, or otherwise do things that can cause them to lose focus on you. Never forget: Attention equals income!

One of the most often asked questions is, "Where do I find the people to be on the teleseminar?" There are a thousand places to find them, and it is often easier for people to say yes to you for a teleseminar because they feel anonymous, they feel they can drop off at any time without being rude or the like. If you are just starting this process, begin by going to your inactive client list. Send these people an e-mail, a postcard, or give them a phone call and invite them to the teleseminar.

Another powerful tool that you should be leveraging is your e-mail list. Send an e-mail to your newsletter list or client list. Often existing clients will sit on a teleseminar to see what is new and will end up buying more or newer products. Never underestimate how much turnover is occurring in companies with which you have an established relationship and that a new employee may want to become more educated about you and your solution.

If you don't currently have an e-mail list, you need to start building one immediately. Use a service such as Aweber (http://budurl.com/elist) to create e-mail campaigns, store and manage subscribers, stay in compliance with the Can Spam act, and send e-mails to all or part of your list at one time. Direct marketers know that the money is in the list, but many salespeople and companies miss this opportunity to connect. Once you have your list and it is growing, you have multiple opportunities to educate your clients. Don't overwhelm them with e-mail; send something only when you have something important and relevant to say.

Using a service also allows you to set up an autoresponder so that you can send a prescheduled e-mail or group of e-mails at specific intervals to influence prospects predictably over time.

Don't forget to leverage the interviews you are doing for your personal site that we talked about earlier. Chances are very high that you are interviewing people who are interesting and relevant to the audience you are prospecting in. Give them a very interesting, nonthreatening way of engaging with you. Be sure that as you interview your guest on the show, you weave in references to your product or service. At the beginning, introduce yourself and tell people what you do in under 90 seconds. At the end, after you've thanked your guest, you can do a two- to five-minute pitch for your product. It is very easy to edit this out so that you can archive your interviews on your personal web site, or you can just leave the pitches in.

A few do's and don'ts about teleseminars:

- Always call from a corded landline. Cell phones are unreliable, and the last thing you want is to have your call dropped in the middle of your presentation.
- Unless your company has a professional conference service, use a free program such as www.conferencetown .com or www.freeconferencecall.com; both allow you to handle large or small groups and (as of this writing) offer free recording of your call, which you can then download easily to edit and put on your web site.
- If you are interviewing a guest for your list, be sure to ask her if she has a list of questions she'd like you to ask, or create your own list and send it to the guest for review so that she can be well prepared for your interview.
- If your teleseminar is to sell, have a plan. Start with the end in mind: What do you want prospects to do? Then

work backward from there to create a compelling environment for taking action.

GETTING DIGITAL DOESN'T REMOVE YOUR NEED TO GET FACE TO FACE WITH CLIENTS

Although getting digital offers you a lot of opportunity to connect with your clients, sometimes being face to face makes the most sense. Don't miss the opportunity to close the sale when you know being present in person will move the sale forward more productively. The trick is to know the difference, and the hardest thing for you will be to begin determining which works better and when. Be sure to test and document your results, and don't forget: Like all new skills, your success will grow as your experience with the new technology grows.

Being digital extends your reach and allows you to prospect many more people at once. It allows people to drop their guard just a little; it sets you apart from your competitors, and it allows you to be much more persuasive and productive than individual phone calls or cold calls alone.

If you'd like some good examples of how I use teleseminars and Webinars, go to www.boldapproach.com/replay and listen to me interview some of the most exceptional people in sales and marketing. Not only will you learn more about how to do teleseminars—you'll learn a lot more about how to sell when it feels like nobody's buying.

RESOURCES

www.ustream.tv

Use to create live video presentation rooms free. Sell from your Web camera.

www.sliderocket.com

Automate your PowerPoint presentations online.

5

GET CREATIVE

OPEN NEW DOORS IN NEW WAYS

Innovation increases compensation.

— Dave Lakhani

I know—you are waiting for me to tell you about the time I sent someone a shoe and a note that said something about getting my foot in the door, right? Well, I've never sent shoes; I've always been more creative and wanted to be more original than that. And I want you to be original and relevant too ... but I want you to set aside your old thinking and prejudices for a while.

Creativity in sales is about making it easier to get to yes and to have a little fun with your prospects along the way.

SIX DEGREES TO THE INFLUENCER

As it becomes increasingly difficult to get through to the proper decision makers, you must cast a wider net. Casting a wider net means reaching deeper into and wider across organizations so that you can reach and influence the real decision makers. It also means that you are now managing multiple relationships in which everyone has a need that has to be met.

A mistake I see salespeople making over and over again is that they fail to think about the needs of the people who separate them from the decision makers. What is in it for the person you are talking to that would cause them to say yes to giving you more information or even to putting your call through? The purpose of talking to gatekeepers is not to circumvent them; it is to woo them well enough that they feel committed to your success. It is also to make them feel important due to the position they hold. Being a little subservient to the person who holds the keys to the next door in the kingdom just makes good sense.

The next set of people that you must think about persuading and influencing are those influencers who are not decision makers but whose opinion matters to the person who does make decisions. It is very important to get them emotionally on your side so that when the time comes, they will do more than their fair share of promoting you when you aren't there.

HOW TO REACH THE UNREACHABLE

Consistency of effort is the key to success in reaching people who are avoiding your calls or who have said, "Not right now." Consistency breeds familiarity. As you already learned, people are more likely to say yes to things that seem familiar to them. The interesting thing is that the comfort bred by familiarity is what causes people to choose brands they've never used before; it is what makes them defend brands or talk about products they've never used in a category, because they've heard about them often enough that they simply recommend them so that they can be helpful to others.

In his book *The Ultimate Sales Machine* (Portfolio, 2007), Chet Holmes talks about his proprietary concept of The Dream 100™—that is, those top 100 clients you'd love to have, the ones that if you got even a fraction of them would make your business. He goes on to talk about a strategy he uses with direct mail to regularly keep in touch with these companies, to move the sales process forward and increase their desire. Chet's book is very good and I strongly recommend reading it.

I want you to take Chet's idea a little further, though; I want you to create a list of not only your top prospects but also of those people who influence those prospects—the people who could help you influence them. And then I want you to get creative:

1. Ask yourself this question: What is important to the person influencing this decision maker? It might be that you are making his job easier or that you are making her look good by saving money. It may be that you are appealing to his vanity or ego by elevating his status. Whatever it is, you need to make a note about what you are going to talk about to create a conversation where one does not exist.

2. Create a conversation around that core idea; talk to the influencer with the intention of getting it to be *her* idea to connect you with the decision maker. Let her bring the idea to the table for you or with you, to reduce resistance.

3. Find out ways you can ethically induce or reasonably reward the influencer's behavior (I'll talk about this more in a minute). Conditioning the influencer to take action by rewarding him for good behavior is one of the most powerful things you can do to get people to support you consistently.

4. Once you start the conversation, if the influencer doesn't make the transition naturally, ask for her help in reaching the decision maker. Your goal is to get the influencer to not only influence but to position you as a respected authority with whom the decision maker should speak.

5. Reward the influencer's behavior after the fact. If you close the deal, thank him by giving him a token of your appreciation—something as simple as a tasteful gift basket, or if you are in town, a meal for him or all the influencers who helped along the way.

Remember the influencers at important times and drop them notes or give them a call. If you don't close the deal and the business goes someplace else, move them to a list of people who get less frequent but reasonably consistent contact. Make them know you care and that you are still interested in them. This is important because you never know when the purchase that was made will not work out or when the influencer will move to another position where he can recommend you.

Let's talk about the ethical inducement for a moment. *Inducement* is a very dangerous word to use in a sales book, because of the implications of bribery and the high-profile cases of bribery that have occurred from government to the boardroom.

An *ethical inducement* is nothing more than giving people something of value to them to get them to do something else. The act may be overt, with obvious cause and effect—for instance, I buy you dinner so you'll be more inclined to like me. Or the act may be more covert—I buy you dinner and at the dinner buy you your favorite wine or dessert in order to psychologically move you closer to liking or preferring me. Both acts have the same effect—I'm giving you something, hoping to initiate the Law of Reciprocation, which says that if I give you something first you are more inclined to give me something in return.

One of the keys to understanding what can work as an ethical inducement is to understand how much a new client is worth to you over time and what percentage of people who you induce will ultimately buy. Many people talk about lifetime value of a customer and always say, "If I could make $1500 over the next three years from a client, I'd happily spend $100 to get that client." The problem is that they don't take into consideration the real cost of getting that client, which includes the cost of offering an inducement to all the people who don't buy. So, if you solicit 100 people and it costs you $100 and you give them each a $5 Starbucks card, your cost for the mailing is $1.50 per person, and your conversion rate is 10 percent, that means that your actual cost per closed customer is $65 (Costs $5 + $1.50 = $6.50 × 100 prospects = $650/10 closed prospects = $65). If your client is worth $100 a year, it can still be a losing proposition, depending on hard costs of the product or delivering the service and overhead. It is very important to understand metrics before you rush into expensive ethical inducements.

However, there are many things you can do to keep costs in line. Create a valuable white paper, create a video demonstrating something important, pay a small honorarium to someone (if you can't get them for free to speak on your teleseminar). Or give a gift once a month to someone whose name is pulled from a hat of names of people subscribed to your newsletter or who have participated in a Webinar. Very popular gifts are iPod Nanos, cameras, dinner gift certificates, Omaha Steaks, and Amazon gift certificates. It is also very easy to get autographed copies of books from authors like me that people love a chance to win.

CREATE A DRIP CAMPAIGN

By understanding how to motivate those influencers who are impacting your top 100 clients, you now have a very strong list of people you can cultivate over time. Sales often happen when visibility meets need, and you want to be sure you are seen when need strikes. A *drip campaign* allows you to create tremendous top-of-mind awareness so that you move to consideration whenever a need for your product or service arises.

Drip campaigns simply involve systematically and consistently dripping some sales message on the person you are attempting to influence until that person is ready to buy. At that moment you should have very high top-of-mind awareness, so if you've provided the prospect with very high value and your product is a good fit for his needs, there is a very high likelihood that he'll say yes to exploring further with you or to reach out proactively when he has a need.

The goal for a drip campaign is to get something in the hand of the influencer and the person you are hoping to influence every four to five weeks. Ideally you'll stagger the effort so that one of the two people is getting something from you every two to three weeks. The staggered strategy allows for a higher likelihood of one or the other initiating a conversation in the shortest period of time.

Here is a look at a drip campaign that I use to influence sales directors and meeting planners—prime decision makers who can hire me. I know I can spend up to $125 per person on my list of 100 people and their subordinates to get a sale that will net me a minimum of $15,000. At the end of the day, if I do this program for a year and only one person buys from me, I'm still $2500 ahead and I've invested in creating massive awareness in the other 99 people.

Drip 1. Phone call introducing myself in person when possible or via voice mail if not. I leave a very professional message and let prospects know that I'm sending them something that I think they'll find useful in opening doors and that they are free to use it with their salespeople if they like. I warn them that it isn't for everyone and only the most innovative, out-of-the-box thinkers will understand how to use it right away. I also reassure them that from my research about them and their company, I suspect they'll know what to do with it right away. At the end of the phone call I send them a big red ball from www.sendaball.com. Sendaball does something very interesting: They mail a 10-inch vinyl child's ball through the postal service with only stamps on it, no packaging, and they handwrite your personal message on it. These mailings get attention. If the ball is flat or undelivered, they replace it free. Here's what my ball says: "It takes big balls to hire Dave Lakhani for your next event—here's one! I've created a special video for you at *(insert video link here)*; please watch it today and I'll show you how I can add great impact to your next event. Call my cell anytime, 208-863-XXXX, with questions —Dave. P.S. If you said to yourself, 'Oh my heck, I can't believe what I'm holding,' you really need to call now!"

I always follow up this drip with a phone call a day or so after I'm confident the ball has arrived or on the day that they click the budurl.com link to the video that I created for them. A nice trick is to include their name as the name of your link so it would look like this: http://budurl.com/*their-name*. It is a nice personalization.

Drip 2. If I haven't heard back from them after Drip 1, I'll send them my media kit, which includes a personally inscribed and signed book. The media package comes in a wrapped gift box inside a FedEx or Priority Mail box. I want them to feel like I'm giving them a valuable gift; this is my ethical inducement.

Drip 3. I send them a DVD of me presenting an hour of material and a facilitator's guide and instruction so that they can use the DVD to deliver a one hour of training to their team.

Drip 4. I send a postcard from a tropical locale that says, "The extra money your team will make will get a lot more of these when you hire Dave Lakhani for your next event. Call me on my cell phone: 208-863-XXXX.

Drip 5. I send a special report or white paper I've created that they will find useful.

Drip 6. I send them a video e-mail from me talking to them about how excited I am that we are able to continue our dialogue and let them know that I'm still looking forward to speaking with them about their next event. I recap what I've sent them so far and I ask the question, "If your sales-people were this consistent about following up with your top prospects, what do you think would happen? If you'd like to know my results, give a call and I'll show you how to personalize this process to your organization; it would be my pleasure to give you this gift that I typically charge $5000 to do." Then I give them my direct line again and tell them to be sure and watch for what is coming next.

Drip 7. I research them on the Internet and try to find something interesting about them. I also try to find a picture of them. I then have both reprinted on a giant oversized color postcard and send it to them. If possible I want their picture to fill up the front of the postcard. People have to read things that have their faces on them. If I can't find anything about them, then I'll try to find something about the company that they are proud of. If I can't find their picture or anything about them, I'll put "Congratulations" at the top of the card and then their logo underneath; I'll then use the thing that they were proud of or bragging about on their web site on the back of the card and tell them how cool it is. I'll tell them I still want to speak at their next event and invite them to call me. I use www.postcardbuilder.com to create and mail my customized postcard.

Drip 8. I send them a tin of Altoids® breath mints with a note that says, "Like Altoids, Dave's message is curiously strong. The first time you experience it, you'll never forget the difference, and the experience will leave you refreshed and ready to embrace your clients confidently, profitably, in a whole new way. Go ahead pop one in and give me a call! Oh, by the way, I've included an audio CD of my last talk for XYZ Company; I thought you'd enjoy some of the profit-producing tips I shared with them, and I've taken the liberty to include testimonials from three people I think you'll respect *(I include high-profile clients)*. I look forward to helping your sales team become curiously strong as well."

Drip 9. I send a handwritten birthday card. Inside I say, "Happy Birthday! Just nine short months ago working with you on your next event was a dream, but today is your birthday—welcome to the world of sales success! I'll be calling to wish you a happy birthday shortly; waiting for you to get in touch will be hard but a labor I can live with! I look forward to sharing many more birthdays together. By the way, I've included a gift I think you'll enjoy. Have a great birthday!" I then include an autographed copy of my second book. This is another ethical inducement that moves them farther down the path of awareness.

Drip 10. I send another DVD of me giving a presentation, this time to a huge crowd of 2000+ people who are going crazy. I include a handwritten note that says, "This is what I want to do at your event. Let's do it together; give me a call." I also send them a video e-mail describing about how much I respect them and how much I want to work with them. I include links to video testimonials.

Drip 11. I send a funny fax. The body of the fax reads:

I'm sending you this fax to express my concern that I might have offended you and, further, to offer my most sincere apologies for my transgression. I'd like to formally offer my apologies, so please simply circle the paragraph below that applies to my transgression so that I can make amends appropriately.

DAVE, YOU OFFENDED ME, AND THE PARAGRAPHS CIRCLED BELOW APPLY SPECIFICALLY TO YOU!

The fact that you even exist offends me. You are the single most repugnant and benighted individual I've had the personal misfortune of descrying in the whole of my existence. Not only do I want you to never call me again, but I implore you on all

(continued)

(continued)

levels to cease and desist before you become the bane of my existence in its entirety and spend the rest of your life rotting in a Turkish men's prison.

☐ I find you not only offensive but annoying. Not only will I never call you to accept your drossy apology, but I will also not accept your call. Never call me again.

☐ Okay, give me a call at _____ am/pm on _____, and with sufficient groveling and truckling I may accept your apology.

☐ Umm, did you eat a lot of paint chips as a child, you psychotic freak of nature? I never got your call or I would have immediately returned it. Please call me after your next visit to the "doctor" to discuss your mental condition.

☐ This fax is the single best reason anyone has ever given me to call them, and rather than fax this back to you, I'll call you right now at *<insert cell number>*. (This paragraph requires no circling unless you are bored or have OCD.) Call anytime—I *will* accept your call.

Again, I apologize for any oversight, offense, or olfactory intrusion and look forward to communing soon.

Yours in humble supplication,
Dave

Drip 12. I send an obituary printed out on newsprint-style paper in a hand-addressed envelope. The return address is "Lakhani Family," with my home address as the return address, and the envelope is marked *Personal*. The obituary reads:

After a long and courageous battle with lack of connection syndrome, Dave Lakhani gave up the fight and joined the scores of other sales training specialists who desperately wanted to connect with *<prospect's name>* to help him achieve accelerated results and produce the ultimate sales event.

Lakhani left a note that said he would attempt to communicate from the Great Void once a quarter by providing ongoing educational information in the form of videos and communications sent via his personal communication devices in hopes that in some foreseeable future he'll be able to reconnect in person.

Lakhani is survived by a hundred other less committed and less creative speakers who will be contacting you shortly. They'll send you unexpected, unwanted irrelevant communications in hopes that they'll get lucky enough to catch you on the day that you are desperate and need their help. They'll even leave messages full of platitudes and well wishes. But in all their attempts, they'll never be able to achieve what Dave Lakhani was able to accomplish in one phone call.

You can send your condolences by calling 208-863-XXXX. Dave's personal afterworld answering system will attempt to pass on your attempt to contact him in the Great Beyond.

It is in these moments that we realize how terrible a thing a relationship is to waste.

On the obituary I handwrite, "Dave really wanted to work with you! Please call 208-863-XXXX for his final message to you."

The example you just read is a drip campaign designed to influence a decision maker over 12–14 months. In addition to this campaign, there is a subcampaign that goes on with the influencers. I don't send them the high-cost gifts, books, balls, and so on; I know that those gifts will be seen or passed on by the influencers. Instead, I send them simple things like white papers, information packages, links to videos, copies of my talks on DVD with a bag of microwavable popcorn, and a note encouraging them to enjoy the popcorn with the movie.

I'll also send them candy from their youth—things they probably haven't seen for a very long time, such as Zotts, bottlecaps, bubble-gum cigars, candy lipstick, Pop Rocks, Big Hunk, or whatever you or your client finds nostalgic that ties in with your mailing. I include a note with the message: "Remember how good this candy was when you were a kid? You can still taste them and they leave you with a special feeling all these years later. That's what it is like when you and your team work with Dave Lakhani. By the way, a great resource for these candies is www.candycrate.com."

The goal of the campaign is to create high top-of-mind awareness and to keep me in the minds of people who can help me get hired or who can hire me. I also want to demonstrate that I've put some thought into engaging them and encourage them to talk.

If at any time during this process they engage me, I change the tone of the contacts to reflect what we've discussed. If they hire me I stop this process and move them into my client management process and begin the process of turning them into a fan for life.

You may be reading this and saying that the process I just laid out makes sense for someone who is a speaker, but "That wouldn't work in my industry." I've heard it a million times. If you sit down and brainstorm with your team, you'll find a 12- to 14-part process that makes sense to you. You'll find the right tie-ins and the right messages. It is simply impossible for me to give enough examples here to cover all possibilities, so stretch your imagination and test.

LUMPY OR DIMENSIONAL MAIL

Letters that contain something in them get opened. Priority Mail through the Post Office and FedEx boxes get opened. Mail that includes something inside it to induce people to open it to see what it contains is often referred to as *lumpy mail* or *dimensional mail*. In addition to including something that people will want to see, whatever you include inside is a transformational mechanism, a device that allows you to connect one thought to another. It also acts as an anchor, a reminder of who you are and where it came from. You'll be tempted to include the printed pens, calendars, or the like that you've spent a lot of money on, but those are rarely the right choice. A better choice is something odd or unexpected that ties in with your product or your message. Or, if you can give a sample of your product, that can be very powerful as well.

The goal of this mailing is to open a door, to get someone to recognize you when you call, to remember you. Again, think outside the box. Here are a few of the things I've mailed or helped clients mail with great success:

- Poker chips with a message about betting on the future
- Candy, reminding people of the nostalgia of their youth
- Bank bags containing my direct mail piece; the postage goes right on the bag
- Kid's toy balls, www.sendaball.com
- Cell phones with a note to turn the phone on at a specific time and that they'd receive a very special phone call
- MP3 players, engraved, containing individual messages
- Piggy banks with a message about savings
- Chess pieces with a message about strategy
- Tarot cards with a message about trying to predict the future
- Hourglasses with a message about running out of time to replace software
- Pocket knives with a message about cutting through red tape
- An abacus, to an accountant asking him if he'd trade it for his calculator and if not, why he was still not using a forms-printing solution
- Clown nose and glasses, a disguise from a mystery shopping company for the managers of a chain that weren't using mystery shoppers so the managers wouldn't be recognized while they were walking around trying to do the job of a real mystery shopper

The list goes on and on. There is no end to what you can connect to what you are selling. It doesn't have to be expensive. Many of the things I've mailed, I purchased at the dollar store; there is some great stuff there that mails very nicely.

WAIT—THERE IS MORE THAN PHYSICAL MAIL!

It isn't only about physical mail. Another tool I've used with great success is Hollywood Is Calling (www.hollywoodiscalling .com). For $19.95 you can choose from one of dozens of celebrities on their site and have them call and give a 30-second message to your prospect. For $5 you can have a celebrity send a video e-mail to your prospect. The celebrities won't endorse your product, but they will ask the recipient to call you.

Rather than use an overnight service, I'll often send what I want delivered to a local courier service and have them deliver my package by hand. To get more attention, I'll gift-wrap the package. I want it to get delivered *and* opened.

There are other, larger-scale things that you can do if the business is worth it, but you have to be willing to take some chances. For example, you might buy a billboard for a month near the entrance to a company that you want to work with and put the name of the person you want to contact on the billboard, along with your phone number and the message "Can we talk?" I actually did this about 10 years ago and it got the call. In the interest of full disclosure, something this aggressive will make some buyers uncomfortable.

I've hired "picketers" to walk in front of a building holding signs asking a certain person to call me. I've sent a mobile car-wash service to wash a person's car that I wanted to talk to; I had the service person have me on hold on their cell phone when they got there and asked for the prospect, to tell them they needed the keys to their car. The person will always want to know who sent them, thinking it is a mistake. The service person hands the phone to the prospect and I'm on the other end. I explain that I've been trying to find a "clean way" to get their attention, that I'd like to schedule five minutes to talk to them, and I'm going to have their car washed for their effort. Most say yes and have the conversation with me right then. Some say no, and others get offended. Here is the thing, though: When nobody is buying and you can't get through to someone, what do you have to lose by taking the risk? And it is no accident that my company is called Bold Approach. We specialize in getting seen so we can sell.

CREATIVE IS ABOUT BREAKING THROUGH THE CLUTTER AND EARNING ATTENTION

At the end of the day, being creative is about really thinking through how you might engage the attention of a certain person long enough to get him to say yes to engaging with you. Then you'll focus on keeping that person engaged. Too often when it seems that nobody is buying, salespeople get more conservative in their approaches rather than more creative. It is harder to get attention now that it ever has been; you have to be different, you have to step outside the box. You have to be seen as someone who offers something significantly different than the next guy who will walk through the door with a lower price or different feature set.

My challenge to you right now is to stop reading this book, list your top 100 prospects, and ask yourself what you could do, say, offer, or use to ethically induce them to say yes to talking to you. Desperate times call for desperate measures; be creative and be bold and you'll be shocked at how many yeses you get.

SLUMP BUSTER

An Interview with Todd Carlson

The key to networking is never being afraid to ask for help.
— Todd Carlson

Todd Carlson is the director of sales for strategic accounts for the world's largest retail software company. He's also been in sales for more than a decade and has sold everything from dating services to high technology. His track record of success is long and well documented. And he's sold through good times and bad and, in the worst economy of modern times, is having one of his best years. I asked him to share a couple of his keys to success with you.

Dave: *Does cold calling still work, and should salespeople still be doing it?*

Todd: Cold calling into accounts is nearly a futile exercise, yet it still needs to be done, but done with a difference. We just have to target different people that are not being overwhelmed in order to reach the decision makers who typically are today. The only effective way to get to who you need to know is through internal and external networking. Here are some of the targets you'll focus on:

- *Internal networking.* Managers, admin assistants, directors, project managers, and developers—you must penetrate them because they will answer e-mails and calls more often.
- *External networking.* Study your prospect and learn who does business with them and works with people similar to those you are targeting.

For example: I learn who provides noncompeting solutions to their IT teams—POS hardware, payment devices, credit authorization, and so on.

You must get internal and external people to *want to help!* And to get them to help, you must provide value to them (specifically) for them to want to be motivated to help you. The question I always ask myself is, "What's in it for them?"

You have heard of six degrees of separation—but in a specific targeted area, I think we are only two to three people removed from anyone we want to know! We just need to be specific as to who we are targeting to reduce it from three people to two and improve our networking efficiency by 50 percent.

Dave: *What is the biggest change you are seeing as a result of the changing economic landscape?*

Todd: One of the biggest things is transparency. There is a lot more due diligence on both sides of the table now. Both buyer and seller want to know if the other will be around and fiscally viable to provide the products and services and to pay for them.

That is a real competitive advantage for smart salespeople and smart companies. When I sell now I go in prepared to demonstrate the financial viability of our company. I'm ready with financials, I'm ready with any other information they need. I preempt their request and my presentation is completely transparent. The result is that my competition is scrambling to catch up. Companies that have hidden faults behind a well-crafted image are out of the game in no time. Salespeople who try to use subterfuge as a means of covering up weaknesses are out of the game immediately. The sales game has changed, and transparency is the new first rule of the game.

Dave: *I know you are a power networker. How do you make so many good connections?*

Todd: Recently I went to a trade show that featured hundreds of CIOs. One evening there was a sponsored cocktail event at which I knew from some sources that a CIO for a $10 billion retailer was going to be present (and I too had an invitation). I really wanted to get to know this CIO because I'd heard rumors about a project. I had also had a real challenge getting to him. Everywhere I turned, there was a gatekeeper blocking me. At the cocktail party there were over 100 people all wearing small name badges, so finding this CIO was not going to be easy. I was doing my networking—with some people I knew from all the years I have been doing this, and some people became new acquaintances. However, every person that I built good rapport with, I asked them for a huge favor . . . I gave them my card that has my cell phone number on it and told them, "If you see this CIO, please call me immediately; I really need an opportunity to meet him." Unfortunately, my phone never rang. The interesting thing is, I found out that the CIO never showed up to the cocktail party, but when I sent him an e-mail the following week, he actually responded—he had heard from a few sources that I was trying to meet him. It made him feel very important that I put such great effort into meeting him, and now I am furthering a relationship with his company. The key to networking and getting in is to never be afraid to ask for help from anyone.

Dave: *Is this a good market or a bad market to be selling in?*
Todd: For those salespeople who are professionals, who are willing to react to the market and learn the new skills that they need, this market is prime. There is a lot of money that can be made right now.

6

GET PERSUASIVE

UNDERSTAND BUYER PSYCHOLOGY
TO SELL MORE NOW

*There is always a crowd of people in any economy who
will find the money to buy a product or service that makes
their lives easier, their riches more sure, or their job secure.
Pitch your product to the story they tell themselves in their
minds and you'll never have a lack of buyers who will say
yes right now.*

— Dave Lakhani

Every day when I talk to salespeople they tell me how the market has changed—how buyers have changed. They tell me that
if they just had a different widget to sell they'd be able to sell
more. And they couldn't be further from the truth. Your prospect buys on psychological autopilot, and you sell believing
that a superior set of features or benefits will win the day. The
reason you are not selling more right now is that you don't
understand how your clients really buy. They are being conditioned and responding to that conditioning without even
knowing it.

One of the biggest challenges you are likely facing right now is that there is turmoil in your industry or your market. Chances are that you are having more difficulty selling than you have in the past. And reality is that a lot of what you are experiencing is not your fault nor the fault of the economy. The problem you are experiencing is that people accept what they hear over and over as being real and uncontrollable. When you hear that the economy is in the toilet or you hear that your industry is experiencing massive downturns, it is very easy to say, "Well, I need to hunker down and ride this out," when in reality what you need to do is focus on calming down your prospects in the face of fear and mass hysteria. The media and the Internet are intrusive sources of negative information. It is often hard to remember that the people reporting this information are pundits who get paid for sharing bad information. Now, don't get me wrong, it doesn't mean that things are happening or that situations aren't in flux. But it also doesn't mean that the sky is falling or that there is no more business in your sector to be had, because there is always more.

SOMATIC MARKERS AND WHY PEOPLE BUY

Dr. Antonio Damasio first coined the term *somatic marker* to explain (in very simple terms) a set of shorthand messages or cues that we have in our brain that are based on past experiences of reward and punishment. For example, when you were young and riding your bike, if you were chased by a dog and bitten on the ankle, your brain created a series of cues that ultimately said, "Whenever you are riding a bike, watch out for mean dogs." That cuing is often interpreted as "Any dog approaching me on my bike is mean, so I must take protective action." You only need to burn your hand on a stove once to know it is hot and to not intentionally touch it, the shortcut in your brain reminds you. Damasio says that those markers serve to connect an experience or emotion with a required reaction.

That same shorthand, those somatic markers, deeply impact our buying decisions. If you've ever been in technology sales you've probably heard the saying, "Nobody ever got fired for buying IBM," or some equivalent version in your industry. When you hear those things you are hearing that shorthand at work. People automatically look in the direction of their conditioning.

That conditioning does not happen only when we are young, though; every day we are creating new markers for the brands we buy and the kind of people we prefer and adding them to our massive collection of shortcuts. These markers make our lives much easier and tasks predictable. Let me ask you the question, "What do you think of something that has a sticker on it that says 'Made in China'? Does it equate with cheap to you?" To many people it does, and because the brain tends to generalize beliefs, we assume that everything made in China is cheap. The media further creates markers that reinforce the bad news of the day; soon you are creating a whole other set of links that make selling much more difficult. These shortcuts put our prospects into a kind of trance, and you have to break that trance.

BREAKING THE TRANCE

People who get so bogged down by what they read or hear are in a kind of trance, and it is your responsibility to break them of it. If you've been in sales long you've likely heard about hypnosis and neuro-linguistic programming (NLP) as selling tools; though they can be powerful techniques, most people are not skilled enough to use them properly. Hypnotists and practitioners of NLP who attempt to use those modalities to persuade nearly always start with the wrong presupposition and more often than not, they fail. You don't need to induce a trance in people; you need to snap them *out* of the trance they are walking around in before you ever begin to persuade.

Most people walk around in a trance that's induced by either their own beliefs and prejudices or by the media. (By the way, this trance is also often what keeps you from selling more.) With precision and ruthless repetition, ideas are blasted effectively into the minds of the people you hope to influence. The result is that prospects develop ideas, beliefs, and opinions that are not even their own. They simply allow these malicious idea programs to run in their heads. Then, when confronted with information to the contrary or when asked about the subject, they allow the programming to come out of their mouths as their truth when in fact they've often never consciously processed the information. The process is much like that of a stage hypnotist who entrances a willing, participatory audience and plants post-hypnotic suggestions for them to bark like a dog when cued. Over time your prospects have been conditioned about how to act when they hear certain news or purported facts, and they begin running their programs; it is subconscious and reaffirmed by others who repeat the same ideas in agreement back to them. They find reinforcement in whatever ideas seem to support how they feel. Your job is to change their perception.

There are two things that happen that initiate this behavior and thwart your attempts at persuasion.

The first challenge is that most people are *inattentionally blind* to attempts to influence and persuade them by a pervasive media. Inattentional blindness was discovered while researchers were studying repetitive motion injuries in factories. When people do a motion over and over, they often become inattentionally blind to the process, and that is often when accidents happen. We've all experienced inattentional blindness. I'm certain you've had an experience where you got into your car, pulled out of the driveway, and when you put the car in park, you realized that you didn't remember a thing that happened between the time you left home and the time you parked, sometimes miles away. You were in fact inattentionally blind to everything going on around you. Often when people get in accidents in this state they report not seeing or noticing anything until the other vehicle hit them.

We operate regularly in a state of inattentional blindness in relation to media messaging. We simply go blank when the media cue (news, commercials, industry trade magazine articles, pundits at trade shows) is fired, believing that we are tuning out the noise or the messages when in fact they go in and go in deep. And when your prospects need information and haven't consciously formulated an opinion, they reach inside and find the information that seems familiar, or they parrot the message they've heard over and over again. They then trot that message out as though it is a real argument or accurate information. In some cases it may be accurate, but in most cases it is tightly spun messaging designed to get a specific response. Think about your own experience for a moment—think about the kind of car you drive and one you won't, think about the brand of peanut butter you eat and why, think about the type of bathroom tissue you purchase. Those purchases are made unconsciously after repetition combined with experience—and changing that is difficult.

The second challenge is that people believe much of what they think, yet much of what they think is incorrect.

Logical fallacies and cognitive biases plague the thinking of people with whom you interact, and the result is that those biases and fallacies become beliefs. Once a bias or fallacy moves to the belief stage, it becomes very difficult to disprove or dislodge, because people are willing to fight to the end to defend their beliefs.

WIDE AWAKE—PERSUADED—WIDE AWAKE

Good hypnotists and good salespeople know that the fastest way of inducing a new trance is to have the subject become aware of experiences she is already having and to build from there.

And that is also the best place to begin developing rapport with prospects so that you can then move them to a new place of consideration.

Attacking beliefs and competition head on rarely works. Telling people they are wrong almost never works, either, so when you want to change minds, you have to start with where they are. This is especially important when you are trying to move someone away from a supplier with which they've had a long-term relationship.

Many of you know that I grew up in a cult and was active in my youth in recruiting others to the group. We didn't start out by telling people that their beliefs were wrong and that those beliefs would damn them; we started by talking to them about their beliefs, we became curious about how they got where they were, and then we introduced new ideas that were easy to accept. Once they'd accepted a few easy ideas, it wasn't that hard to get them curious, to get them asking us questions. Once they began searching, it wasn't hard to get them to accept that there was an end-time prophet and that there was a specific they should be or live. They woke up out of their trance because they got curious and personal; they felt we had something in common.

CURIOSITY BREAKS THE TRANCE

Once you've broken the trance, once you've gotten your prospects curious, introducing new ideas is relatively simple. You present new ideas by connecting those ideas to the ideas you have in common with your prospects. You make prospects aware of where those ideas, beliefs, brands, products, or services have specific applications with which they can agree. To persuade them, you are simply telling them the same thing: "You'll notice as you slip into the car how easily and comfortably the seat engulfs you. Notice how the control panel is positioned to make access to the navigational system and the entertainment center convenient ... how convenient will that be for you the next time you pull out of the driveway in this car?" Or, in a bigger world view, you might say something like, "Haven't you noticed how, for people like us, things don't seem as dire—that when everyone else is watching for the sky to fall we always seem to look forward to the opportunities to grow? I wonder why that is?" You simply presume how they are and they have to agree—you put them in a position where they have to agree that they think differently. Because no matter how much alike we believe we want to think, our thinking is superior and different.

RESETTING THE TRANCE

Once you've shifted their beliefs or at least gotten them intensely curious enough to consider new possibilities, it is time to reset the trance. This is done through simple storytelling. You elicit what they imagine that the product, service, or widget will do for them, and then have them experience doing that thing by putting themselves in the story. In NLP language they call that *future pacing*—you are having your prospects experience something now and in the future. As they project themselves into the future, they begin to accept the new experience, and the new ideas and new beliefs begin to form. The extent to which you can predict the future—in other words, predict experiences that will occur for them or situations with which they will find themselves involved in the near future—the deeper the trance grows and the more real the beliefs become. And as those beliefs become real, buyer's remorse slips away.

Stop making persuasion harder than it is. You don't need a large arsenal of hypnotic language patterns, complicated metaphors, and deepening tactics that mostly don't work anyway. You simply need to break the trance, tell your story, and collect your rewards.

ELICIT THEIR STORY AND TELL ONE BACK

If you've read any of my other books you've undoubtedly heard me talk about telling stories. I'm going to talk about it again because it is such an important persuasion tool that every salesperson needs to understand.

We tell ourselves stories every day in our heads—stories about what is going on around us. We listen to the stories that people tell us about themselves, about their day, about their experience with our products. And the best salespeople know it's smart to continue to elicit the story because as the story comes out and as we get involved in it, a dual narrative emerges—one that allows the prospect's story about what they need and your story about what you have to become intertwined. When that combining occurs, the occurrences of sales go up dramatically. Prospects can tell when a story feels or seems successful to them, and when they see themselves telling a story in the future about the success of the decisions they make today, they often make the decision. It also allows you to set criteria for buying and to preempt your competition.

Rather than go back through the whole process of creating a story, which I've covered thoroughly in my past books, I'm going to give you the highlights and a link to go and study my business storytelling process via video. But first I want to give you a series of questions that get people talking, that elicit their stories, and I'll tell you what you are listening for with each question:

- I'm curious about your current situation related to X. Can you give me a little background and tell me how you got here? This question encourages prospects to open up and tell a story versus just asking you bullet-point questions. It also opens the door for you to give a narrative back.

- How were you able to determine that the old solution was the right one? What made it work while it was working? Here we are listening for what is important to prospects—what were their criteria for deciding. We are also listening for their decision-making process so that when we tell our story in return, we are able present to their criteria for deciding.
- Tell me more about what you are hoping to accomplish with a new X that you aren't able to with your existing X. Here we are listening for their hopes and dreams, what is it that they are looking for, what they hope to accomplish, how their job will be easier, their life improved, their future actualized. These are critical psychological motivators that you'll use later to enhance desire.
- Are there any challenges or stumbling blocks that you would need to clear up before you begin your implementation? Here we are listening for others that need to be involved; we are determining whether the person with whom we are communicating is the influencer or the decision maker.

RESPONSIVE NARRATIVE

When eliciting narrative, it is very powerful to retell the story in a brief, encapsulated format. The goal is to test prospects' presentation of facts, to watch for their emotions, to see whether the emotion is strong in the places it should be, and to see if there is anything they left out. Often, by shortening what you just heard them say and retelling it, you prompt them to tell you more that they left out the first time.

The core of your story should already be built. You know the features and benefits of your product or service, and you know how it compares to the competition. So your goal is to take in everything you've just heard and tell your story in a way that is congruent with what prospects want to accomplish as a result of working with you:

- Start your story naturally and responsively: "As I was listening to you talk it occurred to me that for you to achieve *X*, a certain series of things would have to be in place in order for you to be successful. When clients successfully implement our product, they experience *XYZ*. I believe that when you have that experience you'd be complete as well. Is that accurate?"
- Use big word pictures to help them understand what you are talking about, and make the word pictures emotional as well. Don't minimize emotions by saying that something was challenging when you can say that "the manufacturing line was shut down for 48 hours and all the employees had to be sent home, paid, while a replacement was trucked in from Nevada." Get them involved in the pain and get them involved in the gain as well. Make them both equally emotional.
- Set buying criteria by explaining how decisions must be made and what constitutes good decisions. Deepen the story by talking about how others who have been successful in the same situation made their decisions and chose you.
- Reinforce your stories with social proof. Talk about—or better, show—how others have benefited from working with you, buying your product, or using your service.
- Lead them to the moral of the story. Good stories have strong morals or are wrapped up with endings that make sense. Make sure yours does as well. Lead them down the path where they must agree to a logical next step. Lead them to a place where they see themselves exploring more with you, to asking for a proposal, or to saying yes to what you are selling.

- Watch a complete description of how to craft and tell your powerful selling story here: http://budurl.com/tellmystory.

I don't want you to take my word for it that stories work; I want you to listen to how people around you talk and especially how your clients and prospects talk. Notice how they relate to one another; the deeper the rapport, the more they speak in stories.

Attention equals income. When you change the prospect's focus from the story they are telling themselves, when you interrupt their conditioning and tell a better story, you create instant change and desire. If you'll take the time to focus on the simple ideas that you just learned and apply them to your sales process every day, you'll sell more every day.

7

GET PAID

GETTING MORE OUT OF EVERY SALE

The best time to sell more is when people are buying.
— Dave Lakhani

One of the fastest ways to make more sales when sales are slumping is to sell more to those people who are buying or to make your offer so irresistible that they must say yes because they'll lose more by saying no.

I know the statement in the preceding paragraph seems very obvious, but often people don't get it. When sales are challenging, people are happy to get a sale, any sale, and they forget to ask for more. But think about it for a minute: When times are challenging and you go to McDonalds, they still ask you if you want to upsize your meal, don't they? They don't presume that you can't afford it or that they were lucky to get your business; they simply follow the process. They make it sound easy to do by showing how little extra you pay for so much extra food. The extra drink and extra fries don't cost them that much more incrementally, so they are adding profit to every sale. They get much higher numbers and much higher profit 30 to 50 cents at a time. You can, too.

UP-SELL THEM THE MINUTE THEY SAY YES

The moment someone has made a buying decision, they have made a decision, an emotional commitment, to do business with you. They are now engaged in the process of receiving the promise of the product or service you sell. They like you and they are much more likely at that moment than any other moment to agree to more.

The up-sell simply means offering them even more for only a small additional fee. It is much easier to say yes to the extended warranty right at that moment than it will be a day from now. It is much easier to buy the year of oil changes and regularly scheduled maintenance for a significant discount right now than it will be a month from now. It is much more compelling to buy the five-station phone system because a prospect's company is growing than it is for them to come back and buy another phone later.

The best up-sells are crafted to give people more value for a very small amount of extra investment. Ideally you'll offer a product that has higher quality, offers an additional feature set, or gives some additional advantage. The following script is one that I've used with variation successfully with a number of clients. Here are several examples.

"We've got your printing order scheduled for delivery this Friday. Before you go, take a look at this. This is the paper we'll print your order on. Because you are handing these out at a trade show you may want to consider this paper instead; it has an aqueous coating so it is slightly slick and the colors will be much more robust, giving you a more attractive piece for only a two cents a sheet additional cost. Would you like to increase the impact of your piece?"

"That is an excellent ring you've chosen. Let me show you something about the baguettes—see how these look small and are overpowered by the center diamond? This is the same diamond with slightly larger baguettes that support the center diamond more fully, giving it better balance. This ring is only $100 more than the first one; would you like this one instead?"

"I know you are going to be very happy with this Omniscan scanner for your point-of-sale systems. The Omniscan2 comes with a protective rubber coating on the handle and body and includes an extra-long cord for reaching larger and heavier items. It is $7 more and tends to last about 20% longer in normal use because of the protective coating and the longer cord. Would you like to upgrade to the Omniscan2 and extend the time between purchases?"

Before CompUSA stores went out of business, I bought all my notebook computers there. I never bought warranties, though, because they just didn't seem sensible. Then one day while I was making my purchase a salesman said, "Would you like to buy the two-year warranty? It is $90 and it covers the battery as well. So basically if you buy the warranty you are getting a new battery at less than half price, and these batteries tend to stop holding their charge as well after about a year." It was a very easy thing to say yes to because it made fiscal sense to me and he touched on a point that always plagued me—batteries that won't hold a charge after a short period of time. I'll bet fewer than 50 percent of the people who bought the warranty as I did ever came in and got their battery; they forgot about it (I didn't, I got a new battery after about 14 months) and the warranty expired, unused. The company made more money, and so did the salesperson who was spiffed on the sale and he was selling a product that most people don't buy. And I would have been much less likely to say yes to a warranty if they offered it later or sent the option home with me in the bag and hoped I'd buy it.

DOWN-SELL THEM THE MINUTE THEY SAY NO

The second best time to sell people is when they say no to your premium offer. When people say no they are often covering another objection that they are not going to share. But when you offer them a different option at a different price or with different terms, they will often say yes. Again, too many people accept the no and don't counter-offer. This is where sales is a numbers game; if you ask everyone who says no to you to reconsider a different proposition, a percentage of them will say yes, so your effort isn't wasted.

When I sold point-of-sale solutions, we often packaged together a program of products and installation. When we didn't win the sale for the hardware, we would immediately offer to break it apart and do the rollout and installation for them. About 10 percent of the people we offered that option to said yes, which made the down-sell quite profitable and got everyone closer to their sales goals.

Be creative in thinking about how you can down-sell. What can you offer? When I teach furniture salespeople how to sell and we cover down-selling, I have them immediately show a lower-priced model from the same manufacturer and a similar-appearing lower-priced model from a different manufacturer. Again, many people will say yes to the option.

Another version of down-selling is to show people a set of options. You give them the option that they say no to, follow that with a very low-priced alternative, and then show them the option you'd like them to take. Many times the contrast between high and low, combined with the timing of the offer, makes them say yes to the midrange down-sell. Test this in your industry and see how it works; you'll likely be surprised at what happens.

Here is what *not* to do, though; Don't ask, "Can I show you a different option or quote you on something else?" Simply do it. Don't ask for permission; have a strategy in place ahead of time and move right into the down-sell if they say no to the initial option. I typically say something like this: "I understand. There is another option that I just thought of that makes a little more sense based on what you've told me," and then I launch right into the down-sell. Not allowing them to wait so that you can try to sell them later increases the likelihood that they'll say yes now. Remember, they've already invested time and energy in talking with you in the first place; unless something is really wrong they will likely hear you out. The worst that happens in up-sells or down-sells is that they say no anyway.

BUNDLE IT UP TO SELL MORE

Bundling—that is, packaging several products or services together—is a very common practice now. However, many salespeople don't think about bundling things that are not already set out in a package. It is important that you think on your feet. If you can offer all the products in a package someone wants while getting rid of others, figure it out and make it happen. People will often spend more to get exactly what they want than what they could get separately. Also, don't be afraid to partner with a competitor or other vendor to create a bundle that wins the business rather than letting it walk away. Sure, it may take a little more work, but that is what you do when you are selling in tough times. You dig deeper, you get more creative—you do what it takes.

CROSS-SELL TO HOT PROSPECTS

I sometimes think I've made more money cross-selling and joint venturing than through any other route as a salesperson, and you can, too. Cross-selling in my definition is getting a personal introduction to a buyer from someone who has the ideal client for me but who is not selling a competitive product, in return for me introducing him to my top clients. Every time I mention this to salespeople, sales managers and top salespeople object: "We don't want to give business to anyone else; we want to sell them as much as we can." "It is too dangerous to give our clients to someone else. What if they then make the same deal with our competitor after they get that client from us?" The list of reasons goes on forever and is completely bogus.

Cross-selling works because you get a very warm, endorsed introduction from a trusted source who transfers his power and credibility with the client to you. Recommendation selling is some of the easiest you can ever do, and because the person who is recommending and endorsing you has something to gain (new clients, your endorsement), he is much more likely to keep mentioning you over time.

Most of the time, simply trading off endorsements is enough to incent the other person, but sometimes giving him a commission on the sale or a gift when you close a sale is what it takes to cement a deal.

I have a very specific process that works for maximizing the value of the call and the endorsement. It goes like this:

1. The person calling on her clients agrees to call during a certain period of time—say, 10:00 A.M. to noon. I agree to not take or make any other calls during that time.

2. When the person calling connects with a client, she tells him that she met someone she thought would be a good connection for whatever area you sell in. She then says that she has that person on the other line and would like to introduce the two of you quickly, and asks if the client can hold for 10 seconds while they are connected. She then calls you and you take the call immediately.

3. The call is connected, and she makes the introduction (this part is key) and suggests that the two of you set up a time to talk in the coming week. This is vital because most prospects will agree with the endorsement by someone they trust. If you wait and say you'll call to set up an appointment, your chances are 50/50 at best that you'll book the appointment. Get the appointment while the person the client respects and trusts is listening.

4. Have the person who is endorsing you say, "I know you two are going to really enjoy knowing each other. Dave is an amazing and knowledgeable resource for X. I appreciate you making the appointment because I've been thinking

about you and how I might be able to help and add some additional value."

5. Have the person who initiated the phone call confirm the appointment one more time, and then you all hang up. Don't let the other person stay on the line with the prospect unless the prospect has a specific question and asks to continue the call. It works better if everyone hangs up, because there is less opportunity for the client to have second thoughts and ask the caller to cancel the appointment.

This process has worked every time I've used it in every industry I've used it in. Let me give you some examples to get you started thinking about how it can work for you:

- A janitorial service could cross-sell with a moving service.
- A car dealer could cross-sell with an insurance company.
- A spa could cross-sell with a jewelry company.
- A computer dealer could cross-sell with a cell phone company.
- A baker could cross-sell with a wedding planner.
- A financial services company could cross-sell with a real estate company.
- A hospice could cross-sell with a medical equipment company.
- A mechanic could cross-sell with a tire store.
- A carpet cleaner could cross-sell with a carpet company.

The great thing about cross-selling is that once the relationship with the partner company is set, that company typically becomes fairly proactive in recommending you to potential clients, too, especially with a little prompting.

A final thought about cross-selling is that you can also do endorsed mailings via both traditional direct mail and e-mail. Typically with e-mail I do it in the form of an article in a newsletter or a very specific, targeted mailing to a core group of buyers, not just people who are seeking information by signing up for an e-mail newsletter. If you do a mailing, it is best if you are able to exchange lists and contact information of the people you mailed to so that you can follow up with them directly shortly after the mailing. I typically offer to pay for the cost of printing and mailing to their list on their letterhead and ask that they do the same, but when I've wanted to partner with someone badly enough, I've paid to mail their offer to my list and paid to mail mine to theirs. If you can, it is always good to write the copy that they'll include so that you are sure that the most important points are made.

This idea of cross-selling can go very deep and can even include reciprocal links on each other's web sites and shared booth space at trade shows. Get creative and think deep, and you'll find many ways to leverage how you can cross-sell.

OVERCOMING OBJECTIONS

There will be many objections to up-selling, down-selling, bundling, and cross-selling, but most of them are nonsense. The biggest reason you won't use these techniques to your benefit is because you are uncomfortable. These kinds of selling techniques require a different line of thinking for most salespeople, and to work they require consistency. You have to offer up-sells and down-sells every time you sell, in order to see the incremental sales. You have to look for opportunities to cross-sell wherever they might exist. And you have to get comfortable with a whole lot of people telling you no. But if you'll do this consistently, you'll be making more sales very quickly and you'll make your goals faster than you ever have before.

Your homework for today is to sit down and figure out one up-sell, one down-sell, one new bundle, and one cross-selling opportunity that you can put together. Get them down on paper and implement them within the next week. Keep track of what happens each time you offer them for the next 90 days and I'll bet you'll be surprised at the results.

8

GET LEVERAGE

THE ART OF MASS INFLUENCE

What you do to one is what you do to everyone.

— Dave Lakhani

This may well be one of the most technical chapters of this book. I'm going to lead you through a process that I've used hundreds of times in hundreds of boardrooms worldwide to close millions of dollars' worth of sales. I'm not going to motivate you or pump you up. I'm going to give you a step-by-step process to create results like never before.

When sales are tough to close, you often get only one chance to make your point. The best way to make it is to present it to as many of an organization's influencers and decision makers as you can, all at once. The challenge for most salespeople is that they try to present and influence to the one or two top decision makers in the room and forget about everyone else. At the end of the day, the presentation you give today is not just about selling the product—it is about offering hope and security to those who'll be implementing and using that product. It is also about creating confidence so that even if there are challenges later, you get to manage the process rather than have to refund money or deal with angry customers. This is the time to create a group of committed supporters.

We've all been there—a conference room filled with expectations and competing agendas and just one person responsible for bringing them together and orchestrating a profitable outcome.

YOU

Selling the room is one of the toughest challenges in sales because even when you've correctly identified the decision maker, you've still got to persuade the influencers and the silo builders. You have to overcome the old relationships and the new ones in which some of the group have already invested emotionally.

It is a little like running the gauntlet in the old cowboy-and-Indian movies.

And though it may be frightening at first, it is actually easier than a one-on-one sale if you understand the basics of mass influence.

POSITION AND PACKAGE YOURSELF

Group judgments are quick and often harsh. You must set yourself up to be accepted immediately by the group rather than have them find you incongruous and pick you apart rather than focus on the solution.

Dress for your presentation. In an age of business casual, a suit stands out and commands authority. It is a uniform and a clear indicator of who is in charge in the room. Use it to subconsciously control your environment from the very beginning.

Develop powerful stories that incorporate the use of testimonials of like businesses or like business problems that you've solved. Make sure that each story has a build-up to conflict and obvious resolution. Demonstrate how you've been personally involved in managing and seeing through the successful implementation.

Use simple PowerPoint slides that quickly and clearly communicate your point. Where possible, provide proof using audio and video to deepen the experience and to set you apart from other salespeople who will bring one-dimensional PowerPoint presentations, if any at all. Remember that PowerPoint was developed for storyboarding, the very powerful technique used by filmmakers and other visual communicators to present messages in easy-to-understand segments. Present your most persuasive segments leading into your close.

Use very precise language. Don't stutter, stammer, or use a lot of filler words. Focus on clarity of communication, creating big, emotional word pictures, and stick to the point. People will make the simplest and most obvious choice provided to them. Lead them to that choice.

DIVIDE AND CONQUER

A basic tenet of mass persuasion is that what you do to one, you do to everyone who is emotionally invested in the outcome of the problem at hand. If you gain the compliance of one person, it is much easier to gain the compliance of the rest of the group.

In every group there is a consensus creator—someone who is the leader in the room and to whom everyone looks for guidance. Own that person and you own the room. Don't be fooled, though; the highest-ranking person in the room is probably *not* the person gathering consensus; the highest-ranking person's job is to simply take the recommendation of the group or be the person who asks hard questions. Identifying the consensus creator is relatively easy; it comes from asking questions and watching the responses.

To identify the consensus creator, lead by asking questions that require identification of a problem on the buyer's part.

Here are a few powerful questions to ask to ferret out the consensus creator:

- Who here has been responsible for gathering the ideas of the group and bringing everything together to date?
- What conclusions have you come to as they relate to the solutions presented so far?
- If you could wave a magic wand and have the perfect solution, what would it be? (Ask this question of everyone in the room individually.)
- When you think about these possibilities, what is most important? (Here is where you will see the consensus creator leap into action.)

Once you see who is taking the lead in creating consensus, you now know who you need to influence. That person becomes your focus. Get buy-in from him and he'll get buy-in from everyone else.

COMMUNICATE AND CONTROL

Reflective listening is key at this stage of the game. Reflect back to the consensus creator what you heard him say that everyone agreed to; get his agreement, along with the group's agreement that you understood them.

Buy-in comes when you present information to a person who is gathering consensus in the way that best represents the consensus that was created. So, when you present an idea or solution, you present it to the consensus creator and ask him if the idea or solution meets his understanding of what was earlier agreed to.

A key point in deeply influencing the consensus creator is acknowledging his power. Ask him to confirm that the idea or solution is what meets the group's needs as identified by the group. Let him bring it to the group and confirm it.

When you are ready to present your most powerful points or ideas, do it not from the front of the room but from the side of the consensus creator. Go and stand next to him; place your hand lightly on his shoulder if he is sitting, or stand directly next to him, shoulder to shoulder, lightly touching or nearly touching, and make your point. Communicate from his vantage point and to the point of view of the rest of the room.

When you partner with the consensus maker, you assume his ability to bring about a conclusion, and you get him emotionally involved with you.

TOUCH AND MOVE TO DEEPEN RAPPORT

In boxing, to *stick and move* is to throw a punch and move.

Similarly, in selling a room, we want to move through the room and make physical contact with people everywhere in the room.

One of the biggest mistakes that salespeople make is not being in physical contact with their audience. Humans crave human contact; it connects you, if only temporarily, and it interrupts people's internal dialogue so that the audience's focus is shifted to you.

When I elicit information from people, I nearly always touch them. One of the best places to do this is on the shoulder and/or the back of the arm, if the person is sitting, or on the elbow if he is standing. I'll often lightly touch the elbow or shoulder and hold the touch while I ask the question; I'll then remove the touch as the person speaks, and then touch him again briefly when I thank him or encapsulate his answer.

The key to touch is not to overdo it. It shouldn't look or feel forced, and it shouldn't be excessive. Just a few brief, natural connections that allow the person to know you are there, that you care about him, and that you are focused on him.

CREATING BUY-IN

Your audience needs to see you as someone like them—someone focused on understanding their needs and someone committed to helping them find a perfect or near-perfect solution.

The audience needs to feel your empathy as they describe the pain and challenges that they've experienced that led them to this point and that they've experienced as they've explored all their options.

They need to accept you as their solution provider.

And you create that acceptance by using a combination of four powerful persuasion tactics:

1. *Leverage social proof.* Social proof involves demonstrating the effectiveness of your solution by showing your audience other people who are doing exactly what you are suggesting. It is much easier for people to make a decision or create a change when they see someone else effectively and profitably doing what they are considering. Demonstrate that you and your solution are trustworthy by showing them your solution in action through testimonials and video and, if necessary or practical, by taking them physically to the location where they can experience your solution in action, allowing them to talk, live, to a customer. Demonstrate your solution so that they can see it in action.

2. *Experience the solution.* The deepest levels of persuasion occur when someone experiences something on her own. Her personal experience overrides experiences reported or explained by others, and her own experience thus becomes reality. Experiential persuasion is personally defendable persuasion. The person experiencing the persuasion will defend her belief to the end. She is emotionally committed to the belief. The sooner you engage the audience by getting them involved in your presentation, the faster you'll sell. Engage the group in discussing how they could see your solution working in their organization. Get the consensus creator to help solidify the ideas. Use brainstorming and creative problem solving to get everyone to develop ways that your product will produce the results they need.

3. *Set the criteria.* Jointly set the criteria by which success will be determined. Setting criteria is powerfully persuasive because it is creating a commitment to how the project will be run and judged in terms of its level of success. You are also leading the process of creating the criteria, and you are able to carefully craft it to be unmatched by your competition. For best results, make the criteria as specific as possible, particularly in areas where your solution has a competitive advantage over another potential supplier.

4. *Create the future now.* Have your audience begin describing, either verbally or in writing and in the present tense, what their organization will look like using your solution as it solves their problem. For example, here's a statement they might use: "Distribution is now delivering all shipments 20 percent faster, with an average daily savings of $500 on shipping." I often frame this as an exercise, and I'll say, "Here is what I'd like to have everyone do: Grab a piece of paper and write down, in the present tense, what your organization would look like after implementing our solution." Then have the audience read their answers out loud, and get the consensus creator involved in narrowing them down to the single most powerful outcome that they would experience by implementing your solution.

By getting buy-in from the participants, you get them to accept you as their solution provider. In this effort you've now created a level of intensity in the room that none of your competitors has. You own the audience, and at this point you'll have to really do something out of line to get them to change their mind about you.

INTENSIFY EMOTIONAL CONNECTEDNESS

Once you've gotten buy-in, reinforce with your audience what you've created together. Start by reviewing the criteria you've developed. Second, deepen the connection by offering to do something in the spirit of collaboration, even though you "know that they still need to see other vendors." Get them to commit to some follow-through actions based on your shared understanding from the presentation. By getting the group engaged in implementing some ideas with you, you get them to fully accept you as their solution provider. You go from demonstrating to them to leading them.

CREATE AND MAINTAIN BUYING PRESSURE

One of the elements that I almost always see missing in selling the room is the structured call to action.

A structured call to action is one that is built around the elements of your pitch to the room that lead to a natural conclusion on the part of the group. It may also include discounts, bonuses for early action, or other incentives to buy.

Buying pressure is initiated by gaining agreement throughout your presentation. The more the buyers agree, the more committed to the solution they become.

Here is what the maintained buying pressure sequence looks like:

1. Gather agreement early that your solution can or will work for your audience.
2. Intensify the pressure by getting them to describe, in the present tense, what the applied solution looks like.
3. Hint that you'll be revealing something that will make this the most obvious choice they've ever made.
4. Overcome objections and gather commitment.
5. Reveal the first bonus, price drop, concession, or the like. Let them know how important it is to develop a relationship (notice I didn't say how important *their business* is) and that you want to demonstrate your commitment to them.

6. Offer them an opportunity to come to a buying decision.
7. If there is resistance, offer any other fast-action bonus items, other price considerations, or special incentives.
8. Close again.
9. If necessary, create a break and bring the most interested people around you so that you can close them individually or as a group and get their commitment to driving the deal forward. Create value for them individually; help them advance their agenda and get their needs fulfilled.
10. Close the group as a whole again with the help of your supporters.

In many corporate organizations, making a decision immediately might not be allowed. They could require that a certain number of vendors be consulted or that the group meet again before making a buying decision in order to compare all their options. If this is the case, you can intensify the buying pressure by taking away some incentives if the decision is not made within a certain period of time. This will often get them to the review stage more quickly. However, don't automatically assume that you can't get a commitment or close in the room; attempting the close and asking for the business are imperative. Allow them to tell you what the rest of the process looks like for them, and then close a next step you can all agree on.

You'll also want to stay in close contact with the key influencers in the room and the consensus creator, to keep the emotional connectedness high.

Primacy and relevancy will play key roles in the decision process when the group considers the alternatives. The solution to which they had the most recent exposure will be the one against which your solution is most often compared, unless it was clearly not a fit. Your job is to be sure that you speak with the buying group or your supporters just before their meeting to review the key points of your solution that they found most compelling.

Since you often won't get the chance to do this in person, I suggest you either do it by phone or by creating a simple video, which you can upload to your web site or to Google Video and send to them. The video should be short and to the point, no more than two or three minutes long; it should go over all the most important points, make comparisons to other solutions you know they are reviewing, and resell them on the value proposition of your solution. That person-to-person connection will often be enough to reengage the emotional connectedness and commitment to your product that will pull you through the review process and have yours come out the obvious solution.

High-quality video can now be created using a simple pocket camera such as the Canon SD1100 that we discussed in an earlier chapter.

BIG EFFORT EQUALS BIGGER REWARDS

Selling to the room requires a lot of preparation, a focused and planned presentation, and often, tremendous amounts of follow-up.

By understanding the process and selling using a proven plan, you'll tip the scales in your favor and you'll stand out in a crowded marketplace full of seemingly similar solutions.

But your professionalism, preparedness, and relevant solution will carry the day.

9

GET THEM
SELLING

IN ECONOMIC SLUMPS, GOOD SALES
MANAGERS EARN THEIR PAY

*Sales managers are the first line of defense against the
slump and slowing sales.*

— Dave Lakhani

When I spoke with Todd Carlson, director of sales for one of
the nation's leading manufacturers of high-end retail store
management software, I asked him how a sales manager's job
changes in challenging times. Todd laughed and said, "Well,
from the salesperson's perspective, it doesn't. Their quota will
still be higher than last year, especially if they made their numbers, and the competition will be fierce. And their sales manager
will tell them that they are expected to make it." He went on to
say that in reality, sales managers have to become more active
in developing strategy and plans with their teams, to avoid
creating unnecessary stress. The role of the sales manager is

---

to create accountability and streamline the bureaucracy that can feel overwhelming at times, especially when companies respond to changes in the marketplace.

In a tough economy or in a rapidly changing market, the job of the sales manager becomes more important than ever. When salespeople get nervous or feel unsure, particularly when a large percentage of their income is at risk, they tend to get unfocused and go in too many directions. Gathering those nervous, scattered energies and bringing them back into focus is crucial.

When salespeople experience slumps, sales managers often think that they simply need a shot of motivation or a good old-fashioned butt kicking to get them going again. Those techniques alone rarely work. What salespeople really need is management.

CALM THEIR NERVES

People management is your biggest job as a sales manager, and that includes calming nerves when times get tough. A salesperson's initial reaction to change is often to negotiate for a change in her quota or a restructuring of her pay to try to maintain financial stasis. Your job is to listen, assess, reassure, refocus, mentor, and monitor progress.

LISTEN

The fastest way to get a slumping salesperson back on track is to listen carefully to that person. Because salespeople are on the front line of customer interaction, they often hear about changes or see them long before management does. One of the things that cause salespeople to overreact to a challenge or to change their focus is not being heard. By listening to them early on, you have an opportunity to determine whether what they are reporting is real, and if it is, you can begin working on a sound strategy for correction. Be sure to apply active listening skills—that is, ask questions, provide encouraging feedback to elicit more information, and respond.

People panic fast when their income is threatened, and they tend to want to share their concern with anyone who will listen. The worst thing you can do is not hear out a salesperson in a meaningful way, because that person will go back to the rest of the sales force and talk to anyone who will listen . . . and he'll do that a lot. And that behavior can mark the beginning of an overall problem in the team.

ASSESS

It is important that you accurately assess what the salesperson is telling you. It may even take you a little time to do the research to see whether the information is accurate. What you do at that very moment will greatly determine the outcome of the interaction. It is important that you ask more questions to get to the core issue. As you well know, often what the salesperson presents as the problem or as the reason for his performance often isn't really the problem. It is your job during the assessment phase is to determine whether the problem the salesperson is presenting or the explanation for his performance is real.

Once you've made your assessment of the situation, you need to develop a plan for moving through the challenge. Often salespeople simply need a little direction for them to find their way back. Or the information they present may turn out to be accurate and it may require a change in course for the company, a redesign of products, or some other solution for which you need to take responsibility. Be quick to take responsibility for things that are not the salesperson's job and put your sales staff back to selling.

Often in the assessment you may discover in the salesperson a fundamental lack of understanding or skill that needs to be addressed. Develop a plan for addressing it and execute that plan with the salesperson.

REASSURE

Reassure the salesperson that she will succeed. Encourage her to share experiences of how she's overcome similar challenges in the past. Share your own experiences and reassure her that the management team is behind her. The more confident your salespeople feel, the faster they can reengage.

Don't forget to give them praise for what they've been doing well and for coming to see you with the challenge.

REFOCUS

The key to success in managing through a slump is keeping the salespeople's eyes on the ball. This involves getting them to focus on core skills that have made them successful up to now. It is getting them to consistently take the actions required to succeed, even when nothing seems to be working.

Walk the salesperson who is having the challenge through a specific process or series of steps. Have him document what he is doing so that you can better evaluate it later. Encourage him to review his successful sales and see what he's left out of this sale. This review of successful sales versus the ones with which he is currently having trouble may be challenging for the salesperson. As one of my mentors said, "It's hard to read the label when you are inside the bottle."

It may take several attempts to get your salespeople back on track, but you can do it; in fact, it is imperative that you do it. Because just like selling to a room, what you do to one salesperson, you do to all salespeople, and the rest of them are watching. Keep refocusing and adjusting where necessary until each salesperson is back on track.

MENTOR

You may find during this process that the salesperson needs assistance on key skills. He might not know how to create a certain outcome. He might not have the skills necessary to interact with a certain level of prospect. At those times you must step in and mentor the salesperson to facilitate success. Or you could assign him a mentor who can help him learn that skill. Whatever is appropriate should happen as quickly as you identify the need. Don't let him struggle too long; that only creates a further downward spiral.

When you discover that one salesperson has a deficiency or that she needs additional skills in a certain area, you may inadvertently discover that your whole team is missing a core or necessary skill. This is the time to train them all at once. If you or someone in your organization has the skill to train them, that training should be initiated immediately. If you need to hire a professional to bring in the new level of training, you should do it as soon as is feasible.

MONITOR PROGRESS

This is where many sales managers fail. They do every other step of the process but then fail to follow through and monitor progress. You must schedule a regular review of the progress once you've worked with a salesperson or your team on getting through a slump. This is especially important if there actually are economic or industry-related factors that are impacting the business and you've initiated brand-new strategies.

Success or failure of your team is up to you. The job of the sales manager is to manage. Every salesperson has numbers to meet, and those numbers roll up to be the number you are expected to meet. Don't let your lack of follow-through cause you to fail, too.

WHEN TIMES ARE CHALLENGING, YOU HAVE
TO THINK DIFFERENTLY

When the economy or the market changes, you have to ask yourself whether you are selling the right thing to the right market. I asked Dwayne Speagle, vice president and founder of The Leavitt Group of Boise, about how they'd changed in response to the challenging economy of 2008 and 2009. He replied, "We started thinking differently; rather than looking in the same box every other insurance broker was looking in, we made sure we stayed outside the box. At the end of the day we were able to create our best year ever by bringing a new tool to existing buyers that no one else wanted to provide."

Start asking yourself today: What else is there that we could be doing that everyone else is not doing? What does no one else in the marketplace want to do that we can? How can we create a new opportunity by combining multiple resources? By simply asking yourself these questions, you begin to develop ideas and solutions that can create sales where everyone else is finding failure. It is that level of diverse thinking that will allow you to succeed in any economy.

One of the questions that Dwayne Speagle asked was, "If you (the business owner) knew what we (the broker) know about insurance, would you buy insurance the same way?" The answer, of course, is no, which led Dwayne's company to a whole new way of educating and selling insurance to their clients.

Brainstorm with your team and with the rest of your executive team and start thinking through what you could do that creates opportunity in the marketplace. Your ideas might be disruptive (we'll talk more about that in a special section at the end of the book), or they could involve simply looking at the way things have always been done and selling to those who don't fall neatly into the categories that your standard procedure supports. Whatever you decide, you must decide quickly and act quickly to succeed, because all good ideas will be copied by your competition very quickly.

DON'T FORGET TO RALLY THE TROOPS

Motivation remains a key factor in keeping your team selling in good times or bad. Providing that motivation is your job as a sales manager. Get creative about what you can do to motivate your people.

One of the most fun things I heard about while researching this book was from Russell Brunson, CEO of DotComSecrets .com. Russell has a salesroom where his salespeople do outbound selling of high-end coaching programs as well as other product sales. To get everyone motivated, he once spread money out all over the floor, then had the salespeople cover themselves in tape and roll all at once across the floor to collect as much money as they could; they got to keep the money they collected. Now, some people will find that odd or say, "I could never do that." Russell's salespeople loved it. But Russell's salespeople regularly outperform most other salespeople in his industry. In fact, as a result of his success, he created a whole new piece of business selling other people's coaching and high-end products for them. Russell used divergent thinking and discovered a whole new product to sell to a new market and solved a problem for many people, simply by thinking differently.

Think about what you can do to motivate your sales team right now. Here is a small list of things, big and small, that can make a difference in motivating them:

- Cook them breakfast at work. I've done this at several companies I've worked for. It is very easy and only takes a camp stove or two, some eggs, bacon, orange juice, and coffee, and people love it. You then tell them to go do something unexpected for their clients today.
- Create a sales contest for the day, the month, or the quarter.
- Give a cash bonus to someone who did something exceptional on your team. It doesn't have to be much; a $50 or $100 bill given to someone who excels does wonders.
- Create a President's Club with your CEO. Set criteria for salespeople to make it into the club. The criteria could

be that they meet quota every month or quarter, or that they exceed their quota by a certain percentage. Make the membership rewarding. Give them a plaque or ring or some other way of being identified as a star.

- Create a low-performers award. In one organization where I was director of sales, we had an "In the Tank" award for the person who sold the least in a defined period. If one salesperson was under the minimum, he won; if several people were under the minimum, the lowest performer won. The award was a toilet seat that hung on their cubical wall for a week. No one wanted to win that award!
- Buy milkshakes for everyone when they achieve a particular goal.
- Create a contest where you shave your head if your salespeople reach a very big goal. (Take a look at my picture; it works . . . and it can stick!)

There are a thousand ways you can motivate your sales team; you just have to think about what you are trying to accomplish. It doesn't take a lease on a car or a Rolex. Often, being recognized in the office newsletter and getting a gift certificate for dinner and movie tickets are enough incentive to get people excited about tomorrow.

Whatever you decide to do, it is important that you focus on creating newer and better results for your team and for your bottom line. A sales manager's job is one of the toughest in a company. You are a hero when sales are great and under tremendous pressure when they aren't. The trick is to be sure that your team is on track to support you and that you've strengthened the weak links.

One final thought: In challenging times, after you've provided all the help you can and you have one or two salespeople who are just not responding, you need to cut the strings sooner than later, and here's why. Those people you keep carrying encourage your higher-level performers to do worse, because they see you coddling the weak. Cut your losses fast. And typically where there is flux in the market or the economy, there are a lot of good salespeople on the street looking for work, or they can be recruited away from companies that are not as stable as yours.

In challenging times, good sales managers earn their keep. This is your time to shine and your time to help your team excel. In many ways, this is exactly the opportunity you've been waiting for. Step up and lead your team to new heights and create new opportunities in a market everyone else fears. If you do, you'll make yourself invaluable.

SLUMP BUSTER

FOR SALES MANAGERS AND CEOS: AN INTERVIEW WITH DWAYNE SPEAGLE

I look for every way I can find to stay out of the box.
— Dwayne Speagle

I recently spoke with Dwayne Speagle, vice president and founder of The Leavitt Group of Boise, Inc. When I talked to him about what he did differently in response to the challenging economy of 2008–2009, he said, "We kept the same focus and expectation on sales as we had before the downturn. We thought outside the box and created new programs that suited a new target market we had identified. We presented a new solution to existing buyers that no one else was willing to provide. The result was that we had our biggest sales year in what some people say was the worst economy we've seen since the Great Depression."

Dwayne also talked about what else he and his company did to react to the changing economy and marketplace:

- They outsourced what they didn't do well.
- They restructured their internal sales team to allow the people on the team to focus on what they were best at.
- They created salespeople and support staff who were specialists versus generalists. They started having product specialists work on specific accounts, and business grew.
- They restructured compensation packages so that sales and support were compensated for the salesperson's effort, thus creating a new level of teamwork that hadn't existed before.
- They started asking different questions in their industry, such as "Would you buy insurance differently if you knew what we know?"

Dwayne told me, "By taking what everyone in our industry considers a revolutionary and scary approach, we were able to grow and have our best year ever. Another way we broke with tradition in our industry is that we made the decision to hire the best people we found, no matter the economy. When you hire the right people and keep hiring higher performers, your top performers become your new average performers, and if they don't grow they become the low performers. By increasing the expectations of performance, we are able to have people who are consistently above the norm. Now virtually every time we hire, we raise the bar."

Todd Carlson brought up transparency in his Slump Buster interview, so I asked Dwayne for his thoughts on transparency as a sales tool from a company executive's perspective. Here's what he said:

Transparency is mandatory. We are completely transparent; we show our clients where every dollar in their premium goes and how it was spent. And we ask them to have their current agent do the same thing. The moment you can totally justify every dollar you charge and spend is the moment you earn maximum credibility and trust.

Dwayne also takes a very interesting approach to motivating his team. He shows every employee the cost per hour of running the business, per employee. He then asks them to ask themselves the question, "Is the sale I'm working on worth the amount of premium it will bring in?" Speagle says: "If it costs $55 per hour per employee to run the business and we are going to spend 10 hours to get a piece of business that nets us $200 in premium, that business might not be worth having. We want to focus on higher-value business." By making that decision Speagle says employees have become very conscientious of their time, and that is what has given them the cash to keep spending in a down economy.

At the end of the day, Dwayne's main point for sales managers and CEOs is this:

> "Get outside the box that holds back the rest of your industry, and be sure that your team has skin in the game. The more skin in the game, the more committed they become."

CONTACT DWAYNE

Dwayne teaches business owners how to reduce their insurance premiums. Call him to find out how. 208-672-6144; www .LGBInsurance.com.

10

FINAL
THOUGHTS

The only thing keeping you from going out and trying one more time is you.

— Dave Lakhani

By now, if you've applied even a fraction of what I've shared with you in this book, your ability to sell has increased dramatically and you are certainly more easily generating sales than everyone else around you. Congratulations—you did the one thing that guarantees success every time: You took action.

I know that not everything I shared in this book will work for every person. That isn't the idea. The idea is that you can take what does work and implement that. The rest is just a jumping-off point for your creativity.

If you got this book because you just moved into sales because it was the job you could get, you've just opened a door of possibility that is unbelievable. You are in charge of your destiny, and though that's scary at first, you'll learn to navigate these new waters and you'll step through the door of opportunity of your own creation. Quite simply, there is nothing like knowing that you are in control of your destiny and your earnings. Sell a little more each day and you give yourself a raise each day. That doesn't happen anywhere else in business that I'm aware of.

Slumps and economies change, and the fastest way to change them is *not* to do what everyone else is doing. Look where no one else is looking, sell what no one else is selling. Limit your exposure to the negative news and people who promote it. Surround yourself with positive people who are committed to success no matter what.

If you didn't do the process I outlined in Chapter 0, go back and do it for the next week. If you'll follow the process, you'll jump-start your sales in a way that you won't be able to believe. Reread the stories I've told of the people who've made it, who've reacted to change and who've thrived. Let their examples guide you to your own breakthrough; it is there waiting for you to make it happen.

Your brain is more powerful than you think, so never stop exercising it and improving it. Spend more time learning about selling and about your industry; immerse yourself on the way to work, to appointments, and on the way home. Commit to reading at least one book a month on sales techniques, simply to stay sharp and learn one new approach that you can use. Every new skill you learn today, every new thought you seed your brain with, is a possibility that you'll recognize later without even realizing where it came from. Your brain is powerful that way; it is able to connect things quickly, subconsciously, before you (if ever you) see them.

It is cliché to say it, but make one more call every day before you go home. Do the hard work now and keep it up as things improve and you'll be a superstar. There is no substitute for hard work and proper application of skill. Matt Hoover, who you heard about earlier in the book, told me how he'd win a medal for wrestling in the 2012 Olympics. He said, "I'll win through hard work. Sure, there will be guys there who are stronger than me, but they better be ready for smooth technique. The proper technique applied perfectly will win every time." He could have been talking about sales, because truer words have never been spoken on this topic.

I want you to go back through this book a chapter at a time and develop your own sales turnaround plan. Pick out the ideas you can use and put them down in a process map or strategy outline that you can use. Decide what you'll do and when, and then get busy doing it. Magic only happens when you decide to be a magician.

Face the tough music. It is up to you to be sure that you have a job tomorrow, that you make quota, that your customers are satisfied, that your boss is happy. Get busy doing it, because nothing succeeds better than someone who is throwing his heart into his work. You are your future that you create today; make it the best one you can.

No matter what happens, if your job is downsized or right-sized, if you are laid off or fired, you are only days away from a better opportunity. The very same skills that you apply every day, combined with the strategies you now know, will get you a better opportunity tomorrow. You are in control of your destiny—no one else controls it.

I look forward to hearing of your success. Stop by the web site and leave me a comment or send me an e-mail. Write a great review on Amazon.com for this book so that you can help someone else get the answers they need when they find themselves where you were a few short pages ago. In fact, I'd like to ask you to refer this book to one other person right now. Think of someone you know who is struggling, and tell him or her about the book. I'll appreciate it, and if we meet and I can give you a referral, I will.

I want you to know I'm here for you. In tough times we all have to pull together, so visit my web site at www.boldapproach.com. There you'll find even more resources that you can use to excel. There will be videos, interviews that you can listen to, and blog posts that talk about opportunities—and of course, send me your questions and challenges, and I'll do my best to help you with them.

You are not defined by economies or slumps in sales; you are defined by what you do and what you choose to do when it matters most. Continually refine yourself and you'll continually redefine yourself. Don't waste time on what others think; focus on what you know and focus on where you want to be.

There is no one better for this job than you. There is no better time for you than now. There is no challenge you can't overcome. There is only success in front of you. I believe in you.

Okay, it's time to stop reading and start acting. Get out there and sell something—because there is no better cure for a slump than a sale!

RESOURCES

Bold Approach blog: http://boldapproach.typepad.com

Subliminal persuasion blog: www.subliminalpersuasionbook.com/blog

Call me if you still need help breaking out of the slump. 208-323-2653 or email me at info@boldapproach.com

---

Afterword

An Interview with Matt Hoover, Winner of NBC's *The Biggest Loser* and Olympic Hopeful

Matt Hoover is a speaker, author, and trainer who sells his own services every day. He gets up in the morning, makes sales calls all day, and gets booked. He won season two of NBC's reality show, *The Biggest Loser,* by losing 157 pounds. He is a former wrestler for the University of Iowa who didn't win a national championship in college, so two years ago he entered a national tournament and won. He lost his job in 2009 in the worst economy we've seen in modern times and tripled his income three days later. He's also training to make the Olympic wrestling team in 2012, and he does that on top of meeting his sales goals. Matt is a guy just like you and me who creates exceptional results from the opportunity he sees. This interview with Matt will inspire you to action.

The first period is won by the best technician. The second period is won by the kid in the best shape. The third period is won by the kid with the biggest heart.

— Dan Gable, fabled wrestling coach and Olympic gold medal winner

Dave: *You wrestled for legendary coach and Olympic gold medal winner Dan Gable at the University of Iowa. What lessons have you taken away from wrestling that drive you today?*

Matt: Right. Wrestling taught me a lot of great things. Wrestling in college and taking it to that level really brought to my attention how important it is to be focused on your goals and your objectives. When I was in high school, I was a good wrestler. I won easily. It didn't take a lot of work. I knew I was working harder than everybody else. But it doesn't take a whole lot to be above average when you're around average people with average abilities.

My first workout in college was with a defending national champion, and he beat me up like I had never been beaten up. Coming into college I thought, "I've won two state titles and I was a three-time All-American." I had just come back from the world championships. I thought I was pretty hot stuff.

But I came into the University of Iowa wrestling room, and everybody was hot stuff, so you take it up to another level. Joel beat on me for about two hours, and at the end of practice, when I was sweating and dying, he leaned down in my face and said, "Welcome to college."

Right then, I knew I had to take it up another notch in my work ethic and my focus, because it doesn't matter how good I used to be. What matters is what

you are doing right now. I think if you take that attitude into sales, you come out and maybe you're
pretty successful. Then you say you want to take it up
another notch and you're get around other really successful people. You realize that you're not at the same
level. It's important to focus on where you want to get
to rather than just saying, "Well, I guess they're just
going to be better than me."

I took that lesson from wrestling that first day and it
stuck with me forever because I realized that no matter
where I'm at, I can always be working harder. There's
someone who has been there that you can learn from.
Here this guy is beating everybody in the nation the
year before, and I get to learn from him. Rather than
being upset about how bad he beat me, I wanted to
learn something.

I started hanging out, watching him work out,
watching what he was doing, and started mimicking
what he did and implementing that. You have to be
willing to study and implement what other successful
people are doing. You can watch everybody and read
every book. I knew Dan Gable was my coach, and he
was the greatest coach in the world, but if I wasn't willing to implement what he was teaching, it wasn't going
to do me a bit of good to be in that environment.

That realization was huge for me. What happened
the first year of wrestling at the University of Iowa
was that I did really well. I lost just two matches my
freshman season, both to guys on my team. You have
to surround yourself with great people. I knew the
toughest competition I was ever going to face was in
my own wrestling room. When I went out there on the
mat against someone else, they didn't have a chance,

because I had it in my mind that I had worked harder, that I had been around the best people, and that I was going to win. And that's what happened.

If you take your eyes off that and start thinking you've made it, that's when you start getting in trouble. That was the exact case for me. I'd think, "Well, heck, I've lost two matches, but I was the national champ this year. I've got this down." And I stopped doing what I had been doing that made me successful, and I bottomed out in a hurry. It just keeps coming back to that—it's not what you've done, it's what you're doing. I just can't stress that enough.

Dave: *You were staring success in the face and let it slip away. What happened?*

Matt: Like I said, I had been successful. I knew it; I had tasted success, and then I started to falter a little bit—and it's my own fault. I started thinking I was better than I was. I thought I could go out and drink and party and do the things that other people did. And then it caught up with me. I just got to the point where I felt like I couldn't recover from it, and I started getting injured, I started having grade problems, and then I just quit.

The problem was that quitting. As I said before, once you do it one time, it gets easier and easier. No one ever questions it. When people asked, "Why did you quit wrestling?" I'd say "Well, I was getting hurt," and that's enough. That's good enough for them. But what they didn't hear me say was, I was getting hurt because I was staying out until 3:00 A.M. partying and then going to a workout at 6:00 A.M. You justify it to fit your needs—but it is all excuses. And it's in all areas of your life. Anytime you use an excuse, you're making it fit your needs, and people will believe you. You know the truth and you know whether or not you're doing the right thing.

So, I just quit. I left school. I think I had 12 credits left to graduate. I had the potential to be an All-American. I had it all, then I quit. I spent the next few years of my life thinking about how I should have done this, and I could have done that. I would tell people, "I should have been an All-American." I started living the way that others who I had made fun of and who I passed by on my way up, living and acting just like they were. It took me down in a hurry. I started settling for less and started assuming that I was meant to be miserable and broke. I was meant to not answer the phone, because I knew it was a creditor calling me. That was how I had resigned to live my life. It was a tough way to go.

Dave: *Do you see that happening with salespeople a lot?*

Matt: I do see that a lot. I was in sales before I got onto *The Biggest Loser*. I was the only sales rep in the state of Iowa who carried a particular line of products. You would think that as the only sales rep [for those products] in the state of Iowa, I'd be making ridiculous amounts of money, ridiculous amounts of sales, but I wasn't. I was thinking, "Wow, I got this great job. I work from home, I have all this freedom, what more do I need?" So, rather than chasing down sales, making the phone calls, making the contacts, I thought I'd just let them come to me, because it looked like I was doing everything anyway. How could you not have crazy numbers when your territory is an entire state? So I think that in sales, a lot of people get complacent like I did. They see themselves as doing pretty well. Or they focus on just doing enough to get that bonus; they think, "I want to get my bonus this year so that I

can buy my wife a box of chocolates." You're working for a specific thing that you feel is the measuring
stick that is going to keep your job rather than going
out and saying, "I'm going to break sales records. I'm
going to take my boss's job."

We get complacent and think that there's this pecking
order, and that's where you are, that's where you're going
to be. We think that a person above us or in a supervisor
position, the management or owner, is ultimately always
going to be in charge of us. I think that that mindset
keeps us back from really being where we could be in
sales, because we're just doing what we have to do to get
by rather than doing the extra work to move ahead.

Dave: *So you got a wakeup call one day and you saw an
opportunity to get on NBC's* **The Biggest Loser.** *You
took the opportunity to go on the show and then
you won it. You won because of some core values you
developed for maintaining your life. What are those
core principles that allowed you to lose such a massive amount of weight? How were you able to stick
with it, knowing that you had a monumental task to
complete in a short period of time?*

Matt: The first principle I want to share is that success feels
good.

I enjoy success, I enjoy what comes from it, and I like
to have that feeling. I think too many people just assume
that success is always going to be out of their reach. I've
had success in several different areas of my life, and
I want to continue to have it. For me that means working hard. You have to work to achieve success. It doesn't
simply come to you.

We're all full of potential, but very few people are
willing to work as hard as they need to in order to

fulfill that potential. When you do work hard for success and expect that of yourself, that's when you have success on a regular basis. You must be willing to work to achieve your success; that's the next principle.

Another great principle that I live by is that you're never out of it until you take yourself out of it. And that's true in any arena—sports, family, business. You're not done until you allow yourself to be done. A lot of times we just say, "Well, that's it, my time passed." And every time you say that, those are opportunities that you're not going to get back.

But the majority of the time, you can still do things if you want to. For me, I never had a chance to win the national title in college. So two years ago, I entered a national wrestling tournament, and I won. Now I'm taking that a step further—I've always wanted to be an Olympian. So now I'm going to pursue that and do it. I'm not too old. I've decided that I can do it. I've surrounded myself with good people, good trainers. And I'm working toward that goal to make the 2012 Olympic team. But if I don't make the Olympics, that's fine. At least I'll know, and everyone around me will know, that I gave it everything I had.

So, another guiding principle is to give it everything you've got, and you can't go wrong. It's when you hold back that you'll always wonder, "What if this, what if that?" Try to live your life with no "what-ifs." Make the effort, find out, and then you don't have to be that guy sitting around saying, "I could have been number one, I should have done that."

The minute someone talks to me that way, I kind of shut my ears. I don't want to listen to that, because that means they're not willing to pay the price of greatness.

Dave: *That's very good advice. Now, there have to be some times, I'm sure, when you're wrestling, and certainly when you were on* The Biggest Loser, *when it seems like hard times. It's dire; you're thinking, "I want to quit," or "Things just aren't going my way. I'm trying, but it's not working." What do you do to come back when those things are happening?*

Matt: That does happen. Things get tough, and we start to look around at other options and this and that. And the thing that I learned on *The Biggest Loser*, probably the most important thing of all, was that when you're ready to quit, hang on a little bit longer, because that could be the very moment that everything's about to change. I had a moment on the show when I walked up to a producer and said, "I'm getting ready to throw this challenge, because I'm ready to go home." And he didn't say anything right away. He just looked at me and said, "I've never had you cut out as a quitter." And I thought, "My gosh, that's exactly what got me here—quitting."

And that was it. I decided to stick it out and went from being ready to throw in the towel on $250,000 to winning the show easily and meeting my wife on the show. Now not only did I win the show, but I have a wonderful family, too. That one moment where you're thinking, "This is it—I'm going to throw it in," could be the exact moment you need to turn around and say, "Okay. This is a little tough. I'm going to struggle through this, and great things are going to happen."

Dave: *But that's what a lot of people do, right? They sit around and wait for their moment to come rather than working to make it happen.*

Matt: Yeah, it is—it is about creating your moment. Because if you're waiting for someone else to do it for you, it's never going to be yours. It's going to be someone else's. You've got to work for it, claim it. You've got to take credit for it. When I stuck it out on the show, I was the one doing the work. I was the one learning the lessons. I was the one trying to improve my life. It wasn't my mom and dad losing the weight. It wasn't my mom and dad watching the diet. It was me. We just think that someone else is supposed to do it for us. And that's never going to happen.

You have to get up and get going. Right now is a great example: I lost my job. I was working with this boy who was autistic. The company calls me up one day and says, "You know what? We have to cut back. We're going to lay you off." Now, this is 2009, the worst economy we've seen in my lifetime and very high unemployment. I didn't panic, I didn't get stressed out. I said, "This is one of my moments. I'm supposed to be a speaker and an author. This is what I'm going to do." And I threw myself into it, and *bam*, things started happening. But they happened because I surrounded myself with the right people and was willing to learn from the right people. There are several things that go into that kind of moment that we're talking about.

As Harv Eker says, it's being the right person at the right time in the right place. And when your time comes, you're ready for it. You can't assume you're just going to turn your whole life around if you're not ready for it. And I think that's why I struggled for all those years. They were preparing me for this time in my life.

Dave: *How important is it for you to surround yourself with the right people?*

Matt: Surrounding yourself with the right people is critical. On *The Biggest Loser* I had a great trainer. I knew she was great. I listened to her. I did what she told me. I had workout partners who were willing to work out when I was and willing to work out at the intensity that I was. It made all the difference.

It's surrounding yourself with the right people you can trust. People about whom you can say confidently to yourself, "If I do what this person says, this is going to happen." And then you just believe in it and you do it, not blindly, but seeing the results they've gotten.

If Jillian [the trainer on *The Biggest Loser*] had never trained anybody to lose any weight and said, "Okay, this is what's going to happen. You just trust me to get you $250,000 by doing what I tell you," I'd be like, "Yeah, let's rethink that." In college all my roommates were national champions. I surrounded myself with winners. I put myself in the right position to learn and to be mentored. But then I didn't implement it, and I failed. So it goes back to that thing where you need to be in the right position, be around the right people, but you must implement what they're teaching you.

When I came to your seminar, I could have sat in the back of the room and said, "Great, this guy's got a lot of good stuff. Now I'm going to go home and continue to do it my way." I chose not to do that. I chose to come home, implement it, and *boom*, I'm making money doing what I love by using the principles that I learned from someone who's been there.

Too many times we listen to people who tell us all about weight loss when they weigh 400 pounds, or tell us about business when they've failed at six of them and are failing at a seventh. I don't need to hear what to do from them. I need to hear it from the people who are making it happen, who are successful.

Dave: *One of the excuses that people have at times involves not finding good mentors. Or they've asked some-one to mentor them and they said no. How have you found exceptional mentors, and how did you get them to say yes to helping you?*

Matt: I think what happened for me is, I was willing to do the hard work myself as best I could. And then I was put into positions where I had the opportunity to meet men-tors. And when I met them I was able to show them that I was willing to work. A mentor is someone who's put in the work, who knows how to do things. But they don't want to waste their time with someone who just wants to pick their brain for a minute or get a quick idea that they won't implement. They want to see action.

I consider you one of my mentors. Why would you want to waste your time talking to me if you thought, "This guy just wants my phone number," or "This guy just wants to be able to leverage my connection to do this speaking event"? Or if I just wanted to able to say, "I know Dave Lakhani"? That's useless—useless to both of us. I have to be willing to put that work in and show you that I'm implementing things. I have to call back and say, "You know what" I got this idea—what do you think?" Or "Hey, Dave, I've made some money this week because of the stuff you taught me or the connections I've made." You've got to follow up and let your mentors know that you are putting their ideas into action.

And that's with any type of mentor—you must be willing to follow up and be the one to step up and initiate the conversation. Don't just hope that they'll call you back or that maybe out of luck you'll get a chance. You can't do that. Because there are so many people that want that opportunity that if you just stay by the wayside, you're going to get passed by. It's like everything else you do. My first wrestling coach saw some potential in me. He stuck with me, he watched me never win a match for a whole year, and then he watched me win a couple, and then he watched me go undefeated, because he saw that I wanted to put the work in and he stood by me.

And I think good mentors are willing to do that for people. They say to themselves, "Let's see what this guy's got." And then I went from that great coach to college, where I had another great coach. I've always surrounded myself with great coaches in everything that I've done. And that's when you flourish. And so you surround yourself with great coaches. And then you listen to them and then implement. I can't say that enough—listen and implement what you learn from great coaches.

Because it doesn't matter what you know or how well you can do something right now. It's about learning new techniques. In wrestling, I've always said that technique will always beat strength. I don't care how strong a guy is; when he comes up to wrestle me, he'd better be ready for smooth technique. Because that's what's going to win the match.

I can bench-press a lot of weight. I'm very strong. But when you couple that with technique, you become unbeatable. And that's with anything, once again. A life lesson from sports transfers right over to business. It's the technique. You know? You can be a smooth dresser and all that, but if you don't have the techniques to get where you need to be, it doesn't matter how good you look.

Dave: *Do you have any other advice that you'd give anyone who finds themselves struggling with tough times, or if they find themselves wanting to quit? How can they motivate themselves go one step further?*

Matt: Yeah. The quitting thing first. It's like we talked about earlier. The harder it feels at your bleakest moment may be the very moment when things are about to change. But if you quit, you'll never know. And you'll always go around wondering what would have happened, what could have happened. And that's not a good way to live your life. We always talk about "Put it in the past and forget about it." But when you quit something, it's very hard to just forget about it. When you go out there and try and fail, at least then you can say, "I tried it." When you don't even try to finish something, it's going to haunt you. And you're going to have to deal with that the rest of your life.

As far as the tough times go . . . I'm a product of the tough times. I just lost my job. But within, oh, what was it, three days, I'd tripled my income by losing my job. Sometimes the best thing that can happen to you is something that doesn't look good at the time.

Dave: *By the way, you lost your job in the worst economy that I think you or I or most people reading this book have seen.*

Matt: Yeah, absolutely. And it's a time when unemployment is very high. Because I was forced to lose the safety net, I had to take action. A lot of us hang out in these jobs that we don't like and we feel like we should be somewhere else, but we're afraid to make a change because we have to pay the mortgage. I love speaking. It is my passion. It's what I love to do. But I had that other job because if I didn't have a speaking event this month, at least my mortgage would be paid. We get so complacent and focus on just getting by. We should focus instead on what could happen if we stopped doing that and instead went after our dreams and goals.

If I fall flat on my face, I fall flat on my face. I can't blame anybody but myself now. Before I could blame the economy, but now only I'm responsible for my success. When I lost my job, my wife was a little nervous for a moment. But when she saw me clean out my office, dust off the computer, sit down on a Monday, get dressed for work in dress clothes as though I was going to make sales calls, she thought: "What the heck's going on with this guy?"

Because I think a lot of times the people who work from home, they think no one will know the difference, they can just stay in their pajamas. I get dressed for work at my house. And I have that attitude that if I'm going out, and this is something I learned from you—if you're going out, you'd better show up dressed and acting like the person people expect to see. I implemented that advice and all of a sudden I'm making contacts, I'm talking to people and they are taking me seriously.

Because they're saying, "What's this guy all about? It's a bad economy. Why is this guy wearing $300 jeans?" They notice those things. It's not a bad economy if you're working right. If you're doing it right, this is not a bad time to be in sales.

Dave: *Well, you've certainly proven that. You lost your job and tripled your income.*

Matt: Right, but it comes back to mentoring, listening, and implementing. If I hadn't seen your seminar, I'd be sitting here right now on unemployment, thinking, "Great— now what?" I'd hope I get a speaking engagement and be sitting back and waiting for it to come. As opposed to making 20 phone calls a day. As opposed to getting out there and saying, "This is going to happen for me. I'm going to make it happen." This is going to be my best year ever. I guarantee that this year, in the worst economy that I've ever been in, is going to be my best year ever. Why? Because I'm willing to do the work to make it my best year. I'm not going to listen to people who say this is a bad economy. I don't want to hear it, because it's not true for me.

Dave: *Matt, you are an inspiration. How do people get in touch with you?*

Matt: You can find me at matt-hoover.com, or you can e-mail me at matthoover@bestlifedesign. They can also follow me on Twitter—I'm @biggestlosermat (http://www.twitter.com/biggestlosermat).

CONTRIBUTING AUTHOR ESSAYS

How to Sell More Using Social Media

Dr. Rachna Jain

INTRODUCTION

Social media is one of the fastest-growing methods of online marketing, with more and more Internet users taking part in social media each and every day.

With the rise of social media sites, there has also arisen some confusion about how salespeople should best utilize these sites to generate leads and close more sales.

This is an extremely critical question, because in business, time is money. If you're wasting time or dollars recruiting unqualified customers, you've lost twice—first, in the initial investment of time and money for customer acquisition, and then again in opportunity cost, because your time and dollars could have been spent somewhere else much more profitably. The time spent selling an unqualified prospect can never be regained.

This is why it is vital to understand the various kinds of social sites, the pros and cons of each type of social site, and how to use the social sites most effectively to generate new leads and new business.

Suitable for the topic of selling more in a tough economy, social media, used correctly, is one of the best mechanisms you can employ to build your brand, business, and bottom line.

And there is no better time than now, with Forrester Research indicating that Web 2.0 spending will reach $4.6 billion by 2013.

The rapid rise in social media offers both an opportunity and a challenge. As an opportunity, your business can grow rapidly through proper utilization of social media marketing channels. As a challenge, it can take a lot of time and effort to "crack the code" on using social media effectively and efficiently.

In this chapter, my intention is to help you better understand the social media space and to start the process of implementing social media strategies to improve visibility, credibility, and lead generation.

My company provides turnkey social media marketing and online reputation management for companies, and we've had great success in this process. My goal is to share with you some of the strategies we use to build our clients' businesses, so you can apply them to yours.

Warmly,

Rachna

www.mindsharecorp.com

THE MINDSHARE METHOD[(SM)]

One of the biggest complaints in social media is that there is no way to monetize social media traffic. Fortunately, this idea is completely wrong.

We have developed a proprietary strategy, The Mindshare Method,[(sm)] which focuses on helping clients gain more mindshare and profiting from it.

Mindshare is a concept with several definitions, so let's begin by first defining mindshare. Mindshare is:

- The development of consumer awareness or popularity (Wikipedia).
- Time spent thinking about something (Webster's).
- The process of fostering favorable attitudes toward a product or organization (Bnet.com).
- An informal measure of the amount of talk, mention, or reference an idea, firm, or product generates in public or media (Businessdictionary.com).

Mindshare is created by positive associations with your brand. The more positive associations with your brand, the greater the mindshare your company has.

Social media are an extremely effective mechanism for driving positive associations with your brand.

Remember, whoever gets the most mindshare wins.

Before you begin investing in social media, you must craft your strategy and understand your context. Without these two elements in place, the worst possible thing will happen.

Nothing.

Most people dabble in social media and give up too quickly when it seems like it is not working.

To make social media work best for you, you have to first understand your goals in using it.

As with any sales or marketing strategy, you have to understand where you are, where you are going, and what you want to achieve in order to truly assess the value of any technology, process, or system.

Our approach focuses on four main goals of social media:

1. Branding
2. Traffic generation
3. Engagement
4. Optimization

In a well-run and profitable social media campaign, your social marketing efforts will yield benefits in each of these four dimensions:

1. You will improve your brand and grow your brand recognition.
2. You will optimize your site for valued keyword terms.
3. You will generate traffic to your site.
4. You will engage more ideal clients and prospects.

Ultimately, the combination of these four steps will lead to greater profitability in your business.

Your business will improve if any one of these items is present, but you will experience the fastest growth if all the elements are present.

Strategy and Context

As mentioned previously, the first step in the process of running a profitable social media marketing campaign is to determine your strategy and context.

Strategy refers to the overall plan or big picture of the actions you will take. Strategy is the why; tactics is the how. You must have an underlying plan or strategy; otherwise your social media efforts will be fragmented and disjointed, and you are likely to feel that social media is a waste of time.

With the rapid rise of social media sites (more than 3000 at a recent count), the trend online is toward microfragmentation.

Microfragmentation, in this context, means that your prospects are self-selecting into smaller and smaller groups.

This division into smaller units means that you can target your prospects more efficiently but that it might be more difficult to locate them in the first place.

One methodology we use to help identify how and where to find your best clients online is the DPT profile.

The DPT Profile

Customer DPT refers to customer demographics, psychographics, and technographics.

- *Demographics* refers to observable characteristics—age, educational level, career, income, job title, and the like.
- *Psychographics* refers to inner or motivational traits such as honesty, integrity, happiness, sense of humor, and so on.
- *Technographics*, a term referenced by Charlene Li and Josh Bernoff in their excellent book, *Groundswell*, refers to the likelihood that this prospect will be involved in the social media space.

You must understand your prospects' DPT in order to know how and where to find them within the social media sphere.

Since it is likely that you are familiar with demographics and psychographics, we'll focus a bit more on technographics before moving to the next stage in the process.

Technographics is a method for understanding how likely people are to invest in the social media landscape. This is important to understand, because if your target audience is not involved in social media, you will waste dollars and time trying to find them.

Therefore, it is wise to examine and grasp the various means by which people might be involved in the social media space and to understand how your best clients and customers are taking part in Web 2.0.

Developing a sound strategy now will save you time and effort later.

The technographics process defines people by their level of participation with the social media space. There are six main classifications for social media use:

Creators. They publish Web pages, maintain blogs, and create content for the Web, such as audio and video. Creators make up about 13 percent of online consumers.

Critics. They comment on blogs and post ratings and reviews. They make up about 19 percent of people online.

Collectors. They use RSS and tag Web pages, helping classify content. They make up about 15 percent of online consumers.

Joiners. They use social networking sites and make up about 19 percent of online consumers.

Spectators. This group reads blogs, watches video, and listens to podcasts. They consume information but are not likely to comment on, rate, or create it. This group makes up about 33 percent of online consumers.

Inactives. This group does not participate in social media. In 2007, this group comprised about 52 percent of online consumers.

Though inactives made up the largest category of online users in 2007, their numbers declined to about 42 percent in 2008. This means that more people are starting to adopt social media/Web 2.0 technologies.

One other way to understand this construct is to realize that a vast majority (33 percent) of people online are spectators. This means that they will read blogs, listen to podcasts, and watch videos but might never comment on, critique, or create any content themselves.

This is a useful way to understand why your blog might be getting a lot of traffic but not many comments. It may be that your blog readership is made up of many spectators rather than critics or creators.

It is useful to think about technographics as a method for understanding how likely your target audience is to participate online and in what manner they are likely to do so.

HOW DO PROSPECTS TALK ABOUT THEIR PROBLEMS?

Gaining attention in social media relies on using the same language and terms in your marketing that your prospects use to describe their problems.

There is little else that grabs attention as quickly as the experience of feeling like someone "took the words right out of your mouth"—and this is the strategy you want to use on social sites to get noticed and get attention.

You cannot sell anything until you have captured attention.

But once you have captured attention, you have more opportunities to build desire and interest and to lead the qualified prospect into a sales conversation.

This is why your social media content is crucial and why your content should reflect the exact words and phrases your ideal clients use to describe their struggles and challenges.

How do you know?

Ask. Call your best clients and ask them how they would describe the problems or challenges that led them to hire you. Find out what they were hoping for when buying from you, and find out if they got more value than they expected.

It may be helpful to record these conversations so that you can note exact phrases, statements, and experiences to help you get attention.

You want your prospects to feel that you are speaking directly *to* them. Mastering this skill will mean that your social media promotion will be noticed and remembered.

FINDING YOUR PROSPECTS ONLINE

Once you have identified who you are targeting, it's time to start looking for them online. There are several strategies to help you do this.

First, check your web site logs and conversion tracking. Notice which sites are sending you a lot of traffic and which sites are sending clients who convert, either by signing up for your mailing list or by purchasing directly.

These are likely to be the most well-qualified leads for your business because they have self-selected to receive more information or have actually made a purchase.

Once you notice a pattern or trend in who is sending you traffic, it's time to visit Quantcast.com. Start by typing in your main web site's URL. If your site has been tracked, you will be able to access an extremely detailed analysis of the kinds and types of visitors who come to your site. Most large sites and those that have been online for a long time will show data in Quantcast.com.

If your site is not listed in Quantcast.com, you can add a small tracking code to your site and start collecting Quantcast.com data. Realize, though, that by adding this data to Quantcast.com, your site makeup and traffic rank will be available for anyone who searches.

If your site does not show data in Quantcast.com or you don't prefer to track on your site directly, you can estimate the kinds and types of traffic you get by typing the web site addresses of your top referrers.

When you see who is visiting your top referrers' sites, you'll have a better idea of the kinds of traffic clicking through or coming to your site. Though this is not a perfect representation, getting some data is better than nothing. It is useful to understand the composition and features of your site visitors because you'll have the best luck in social media if you find more people like those who are already visiting your site.

This step is about quantifying, as much as possible, who is visiting your site and trying to find other groups similar in demographic, psychographic, and technographic makeup to your current site visitors.

Once you have identified your customers' DPT, it's time to find them on the various types of social media sites.

THE ELEVEN TYPES OF SOCIAL MEDIA SITES

1. Blog/RSS sites
2. Content-sharing sites
3. Business reputation sites
4. Microblogging platforms
5. Social networking sites
6. Social bookmarking sites
7. Q&A sites
8. Mobile platforms
9. Classified ad sites
10. Special-interest sites
11. Widgets/applications

(Plus there are hybrids of these, too!)

Blog/RSS Sites

The first step to participating in social media is to have your own blog. Having your own, self-hosted blog enables you create and deploy content rapidly and allows you to create a centralized hub or location for all your social media efforts. Blogging is a very powerful, cost-effective, and efficient way to build your social media presence.

Blogs are often ranked very quickly in the search engines, and it is possible to generate tens of thousands of visitors per day from regular, relevant blogging. If you don't have one, setting up your own blog should be the first step in your social media campaign.

If you have a blog that isn't performing as well as you hoped, don't abandon the idea of blogging altogether. Just because it isn't working right now doesn't mean it can't work. We've been able to implement some small changes and adjustments that have resulted in significant traffic and ranking gains. So if your blog isn't performing as it should, tweak it until it does.

Your credibility in social media does rely on you having your own blog.

RSS sharing is a method for rapidly and widely syndicating your content. This is crucial because what good is good content if nobody reads it, right?

By syndicating your content on RSS-sharing sites such as Feedest.com, Feedplex.com, and Feedbomb.com (in addition to others your blog may be automatically updating), you can ensure the widest possible audience for all the content you create and share.

When you focus on skillful syndication of all the content you create, you will be able to create more traffic, more leads, and more business from your blog.

Once your blog is up and running, it's time to examine the other 10 kinds of social sites.

The Content-Sharing Sites

Content-sharing sites, just as the name implies, enable users to upload, trade, and share content. Text or written content is the most widely shared format, but many sites offer (or are adding) audio and video capabilities.

Content-sharing sites are useful for educating prospects and improving search engine optimization around specific keyword terms and phrases and can be useful for generating traffic back to your main web site or blog, especially if there is a strong and relevant call to action.

Examples of content-sharing sites include Squidoo.com, Hubpages.com, Scribd.com, Zimbio.com, Gather.com, and Wetpaint.com.

Content shared on these sites should be original and should focus on speaking directly to your desired target audience. Again, use phrases and terms that are relevant and meaningful to those you seek to reach.

It is common for content-sharing sites to initially rank very well in Google and then to drop off a bit and then reappear after that.

Don't worry about this fluctuation. Sharing meaningful content over time is one of the best ways to generate new leads to your business.

Business Reputation Sites

The business reputation sites are a vital element of your social media efforts because they help you manage and control your online reputation.

Online reputation is one of the easiest things to lose; it takes just a few well-placed blog posts and a little syndication and suddenly your reputation has been trashed.

This happened to a client of ours who was accused of improper business practices. The story spread like wildfire on the Internet and was continually reposted. Within a space of about three days, the client had lost all ranking for his own name and his money-making terms. This meant that whenever anyone searched on his name, they would see the negative publicity.

If this client had better online reputation management before this incident, it would have been easier and faster to recover his online reputation. As it was, we were able to recover his rankings within a few months, which is very respectable—but it is always wise to invest in online reputation management *before* you need it.

The search engines never really forget, so it's vital to share online only what you are willing to have live online forever. Stated another way, this means that you should share online only that information you wouldn't mind everyone knowing about you and your company.

Start by setting up profiles at www.zoominfo.com and www .naymz.com.

Get a lead on what people are saying about you, your company, and your services by setting up custom searches at sites such as www.google.com/alerts, www.keotag.com, and www.serph.com.

The more you can manage and monitor your online reputation, the easier it will be to create an effective online presence and improve your credibility and visibility.

Microblogging Platforms

Microblogging platforms are designed for rapid transmission of short ideas or thoughts to an interested community. Perhaps the most well-known microblogging platform is Twitter.com, though Plurk.com and Jaiku.com are also popular.

Twitter, for instance, has a 140-character limit. It is a good method for expressing yourself with brevity, clarity, and wit. Updates in Twitter are available to anyone who wants to review them, making it a reasonably transparent form of communication.

When using these kinds of microblogging sites, it's vital to remember that everyone can see what you're sharing, so you need to share wisely. If you are using these sites to develop more business, it's important to reach out, connect with others, and respond to conversations. It is also important not to focus too much on yourself (nobody *really* cares what you had for breakfast), and if you don't have anything useful to say, perhaps you should refrain.

It takes a bit of time to find your voice and style on the microblogging platforms, but the effort is time well spent.

As a salesperson, you might use Twitter.com to do rapid market research, send your followers to a survey, name your new product line, or get a great subtitle for your book. You can get minute-by-minute reactions around national events and use your Twitterfeed to create new content and new conversations that are likely to interest your clients.

Social Networking Sites

Social networking sites are sites where you can meet and network with other users. Though most Web 2.0 sites offer social networking capabilities, there are a few sites with social networking and meeting as their main focus.

For salespeople, the two most important sites on which to develop a presence are Facebook.com and LinkedIn.com. Facebook tends to have a more social feel and can be an excellent place to make personal contacts and connections that may lead to new business and opportunities.

LinkedIn, by contrast, is designed primarily for professional networking and, as such, relies heavily on developing and building a network of professional contacts. You can use LinkedIn to follow up on conferences and events. I, for instance, collect business cards at events and then find these people on LinkedIn and add them to my network there. This helps me remember faces and names, and to cement connections much more easily. (It also saves me from having stacks and stacks of business cards, which eventually become overwhelming.)

The other way you can use LinkedIn is for industry research; you can see who has recently joined a company, and you can track the professional accomplishments of people you'd like to connect with. LinkedIn also gives you the option to ask questions and offer advice; these are both great strategies for market research and for positioning yourself as an expert in your industry.

The biggest advantage of social networking sites is that your actions are updated in all your contact's profiles. So, this means that if you post an update or more information in your profile, everyone in your network can view it, if they choose.

This way you have a built-in method for "getting the word out" about new initiatives and developments, and you can do this in an indirect, nonhyped way—which fits very well with the concept of leveraging every opportunity to sell more in tough times.

Social Bookmarking Sites

The social bookmarking sites are best used in two ways: first, as a way to build links back to your site, which increases yoursite's page rank and value, and second, as a way to share your content with a community of readers, some of whom may be tempted to click back through to your main site and learn more.

Examples of social bookmarking sites include www.digg.com, buzz.yahoo.com, www.propeller.com, www.delicious.com, and www.reddit.com. There are many others, but these are some of the most highly visited and well-regarded social bookmarking sites at this time.

These sites get massive amounts of Internet traffic—millions of visitors per day. As a salesperson, it makes sense to have your content linked from these sites, both in terms of search engine benefits and in terms of reach and getting page views.

The best way to use social bookmarking sites effectively is to develop strong, useful, and helpful content, with a strong and provocative title, and to publish the link in the most targeted place. So, for instance, if your company sells lifestyle products, you would write an article that contains useful information, develop a strong and provocative title, and then place it in the lifestyle category of any of the social bookmarking sites.

By taking the time to complete these steps and being focused and strategic in your content creation, you will be able to generate traffic and site visitors from the social bookmarking sites.

The biggest goal here, in terms of selling, is to try to increase the number of prospects you connect with each day and to continue to build your site traffic and blog visitors. When you can "pull" someone from a social media site into your funnel, you can then continue to market and sell to them on an ongoing basis.

So it makes sense that the greater your reach, the more visitors you will have and the greater the likelihood of converting these visitors into customers.

Q&A Sites

Q&A, or answer sites, are another form of content-sharing site. At these sites, users post questions about all kinds of topics and are looking for input and information to answer their questions.

Examples of these kinds of sites are answers.yahoo.com, www.askville.com, www.answerbag.com, and www.yedda.com.

The benefit of using these kinds of sites is that if you sell for a local business, you can target exclusively by geographic region or target area. It is very common to visit any of these sites and find people asking questions about their hometown, seeking references or resources for day spas, restaurants, and other service businesses.

If you sell for a locally based service business, you can easily attract new clients and customers simply by being available and helpful on these Q&A sites.

Most of the answer sites allow you to link to helpful information (such as your own web site!) when answering a question. It is normal and natural that people who like your answer will click through to your site to learn more.

If you sell for a national or online business, the answer sites can send you traffic and links and build your credibility.

We have clients who have tripled their mailing list database size simply by frequent, consistent, and helpful posting on a wide variety of Q&A sites.

Answer sites enable you to build your authority status and presence, especially when you give good information that is helpful and doesn't seem to be overtly self-serving.

Many of our clients repurpose their answers on these Q&A sites into new articles, blog posts, or advice columns on their own sites. Therefore, a one-time investment of time to answer a question can be leveraged into multiple sales and marketing opportunities.

Mobile Platforms

Mobile platforms are one of the fastest-growing segments of social media. As the name indicates, these are sites that focus on sharing content via cellular or mobile phone.

Examples of mobile platform sites include www.mobango .com, www.storyz.com, and www.wadja.com.

The core of social media is choice. Users like to access their movies, music, pictures, and information how and when they want.

Mobile platforms give users this choice; they can carry their favorite music, movies, and pictures with them and access them any time of day or night. In addition, mobile platforms allow for the sharing of relevant and meaningful content with friends or family, which means a single mobile user can influence tens of hundreds of others, simply by sharing media clips.

For the salesperson, mobile platforms represent a large and growing opportunity to further connect with, and assist, your best customers.

Perhaps you can send up-to-the-minute updates or reports by cell phone to your clients who have chosen to receive this information. You can use mobile platforms to send content and give people a chance to consume it on their own terms and in their own way. Because of this time shift (delay between when you provide content and when it might be accessed), it's wisest to focus on providing evergreen content via mobile platforms.

You can use mobile platforms to notify customers about impending sales, discounts, or special events. (You would only text or contact customers who had opted in, so they would, presumably, be glad to hear from you.)

The other way you might use mobile platforms is to offer support, tips, or suggestions to your clients. What if you offered job interview skills and training and then sent brief, supportive updates to your clients via cell phone on the days you knew they were interviewing for a new job? What if you were able to offer "just-in-time" technical support, where frustrated customers could text in that they needed help and would get a call back from a qualified support person within minutes? What if you offered targeted free tips and strategies by text, focused solely on positioning your company as the best choice in your industry?

Current statistics (from emarketer.com) suggest that, in 2007, more than 82 million people used their phones to access social media sites. In 2008, this number rose to 147 million; it is expected to reach 803 million by 2012.

The sooner you utilize mobile platforms, the more you will sell.

Classified Ad Sites

Classified ad sites are another way to generate leads within the social media space. Online classified ads operate similarly to offline classified ads, but online classified ads have much greater reach and last longer than offline ones.

Examples of online classified ad sites include www.usfreeads .com, www.craigslist.com, www.backpage.com, and eBay's classified ads system.

These sites all allow you to generate leads for your business by placing online advertisements. The goal of these online advertisements is that they succinctly and clearly state what is being sold, the benefits of the product or service, and the price.

For salespeople, you can use classified ad sites to target new customers and to reach them cost effectively, since most online classified sites are free or very low cost.

To generate qualified leads, it would be wise to test multiple ads and to target them as specifically as possible.

Focus on one product or service per advertisement. Offer a clear next action or next step the interested person should take. Aim to draw people from the classified ad site to your own blog or web site, and then offer them something valuable for joining your mailing list or submitting an information request form.

Given that the online classifieds reach millions of people each day, it is easy to see how you can use these sites to build your sales pipeline.

Special-Interest Sites

Special-interest sites are social media sites focused on a particular industry, goal, or target audience. These types of sites are good meeting places for people with similar backgrounds, interests, goals, or hobbies.

Examples of special-interest sites are sites created at www .ning.com, an online service that lets you create a social media site for any topic area, as well as www.shelfari.com and www .43things.com.

These sites emphasize the process of gathering like-minded groups of people together. They can be a huge resource for salespeople seeking leads.

Assuming you have targeted your client profile accurately, you should know exactly who you would like to connect with online. Targeted special-interest sites make it easy for you to connect with many people in your target market in one place.

This can improve the efficiency and accuracy of your sales and marketing process. Special-interest sites also enable you to perform multiple levels of market research, because you can learn about the challenges and frustrations of your target market, directly from people in that market, in their own words. You won't need to guess what they think—you'll know.

If your product or service is inherently social in nature (meaning that people will gather to share or talk about it), you can most certainly locate a special-interest social site for your industry.

And, if one doesn't exist, start one yourself. You'll boost your credibility and authority among those you most want to reach and begin a relationship with.

Widgets and Applications

Widgets and applications are relative newcomers to the social media scene. Widgets are simply small pieces of code or text that perform a specific function. Widgets can be used for rapid content syndication and mass deployment across a variety of online platforms.

Widgets can be used as content aggregators, whereby you can pull a group of widgets onto your desktop and get up-to-date reporting on topics of interest to you.

As salespeople, your goal should be to create widgets that continually place you in front of your best customers.

If you want to drive more engagement with your company, one of the best ways to do this is by developing custom widgets and encouraging your clients to download these to their desktops. Consider these types of widgets as a form of direct-to-desktop communication; you can use them to send out relevant, targeted, and highly useful content, information, tips, hints, or strategies that will help your clients invest more often and more frequently in your business.

Applications are similar to widgets but are often a bit more complex. Applications typically require that some code be executed or installed. Perhaps the most recognizable applications are those you see in Facebook.com, which add functionality (or annoyance) to your user experience. Applications that perform functions useful to your clients can be another avenue for generating more leads and customers.

Though the cost of creating applications can be significant, this one-time investment should have ongoing benefits.

CRAFTING A SOCIAL MEDIA STRATEGY TO SELL WHEN NO ONE IS BUYING

Here is your social media strategy plan:

- Determine your strategy and context. How many resources can you devote to social media marketing? How will you measure and quantify your results?
- Determine your ideal client DPT profile.
- Locate your ideal clients online using search engine and traffic data.
- Set up tracking for your blog using www.google.com/analytics.
- Contact your previous clients and determine the exact words and phrases they use to describe the problems for which you sold them solutions.
- Set up alerts for your main keyword phrases and terms using www.google.com/alerts, and set up RSS feeds for your keyword terms (including your name and your company name) at www.serph.com and www.keotag.com.

- Set up your own blog, focusing on yourself and your personal brand and information. I recommend using Wordpress (download for free at www.wordpress.org) and hosting this on your own domain, with your own hosting account. (Stay away from free hosting; you get what you pay for—and free sites don't set the stage for you to be seen as a successful salesperson!)
- Invest some time in reading the terms of service and use for each of the sites you'll be using in the next steps. Taking time to read these ahead of time can shorten your learning curve and keep you from getting banned.
- Develop content for the content-sharing sites, focusing on educating potential clients using descriptions and titles that will speak directly to your target audience.
- Set up profiles on the main business reputation sites, such as www.zoominfo.com and www.naymz.com.
- Set up social bookmarking profiles and judiciously bookmark good content you find on the Web, sometimes including your own.
- Set up profiles on www.facebook.com and www.linkedin .com. On these sites, start reaching out to people you know or have worked with. When you attend meetings, conferences, or trade shows, seek to further the initial contacts you made by finding and connecting with them on these sites. On Facebook, also reach out to people you know socially—it can only help to see and be seen.
- Join www.twitter.com and start following people. Observe how others are using the site, and then start posting updates of your own. On Twitter, be sure to follow @davelakhani for updates and contest opportunities. (And you can find me, @rachnajain.)
- Locate career relevant sections on the Q&A sites (answers. yahoo.com, www.askville.com) and start answering

questions related to your expertise or industry. You can also do this on LinkedIn.

- Make use of the classified ad sites (www.craigslist.com, www .backpages.com) to place small classified ads for your product or service. Collect these to a mailing list or database.
- Explore how you can adopt mobile platforms to serve your sales goals and client service goals.
- Get active on special-interest sites relevant to your industry.

SPECIAL BONUS!

As a special gift for investing in this book, Dave and I want to offer you an opportunity to access free social media training by visiting a special web site we've set up just for this purpose. This is only available to those who have purchased the book, so please don't share this special link with anyone else.

The information and tools in this site will help shorten your learning curve around social media and will help you succeed with your social media efforts.

Get details at this page:

http://www.mindsharecorp.com/blog/book-bonus-registration

You'll need this password: *socialmedialeadgen* to access instructions on signing up for the training.

CONCLUSION

In a difficult economy, it is wise to use every strategy at your disposal to find sources of leads and convert them. With the rapid growth of the Internet, it makes sense to use online methods to seek out and tap into new customer sources.

With more and more of the world stepping onto the Internet, opportunities will continue to grow with the global market. In this broad-based view, one could view social media as a blue ocean strategy for businesses seeking new opportunities and new customers.

As with any other form of selling, social media marketing relies on sound strategy and relevant context for targeting, connecting with, and influencing your target market.

As Dave Lakhani often says, "You have to be seen to sell." And social media offers you, and your company, an unprecedented opportunity for being seen and selling, no matter what the economic conditions.

Social media is not a quick-hit strategy, and it is incorrect to consider it as such. If you choose to invest in social media, you must be consistent and focused to create real and lasting results.

Investing in the social media landscape does require resources, in the form of time or money. This investment is returned multiple times over if you are able to create results.

For most users of social media, results will be incremental rather than exponential. But it doesn't take too many "incremental" gains over time to equal significant impact.

Social media can assist you in lowering the cost of customer acquisition, building your reputation, and growing your visibility and credibility with your target audience.

The question is not whether you should invest in social media. The truth is that you can't afford not to.

Dr. Rachna Jain is the Chief Social Marketer at MindshareCorp.com and lead developer of The Mindshare Method[sm], a social media-based lead generation and profit strategy. A clinical psychologist by training, Dr. Jain focuses on using the most cutting-edge psychological techniques, combined with a deep understanding of human nature and social dynamics, to create social media campaigns that get noticed.

Every business is different. Every business has a unique story. MindshareCorp focus on finding relevant contexts for your story so that it can be seen and heard by those you want to influence.

Using a proprietary combination of social media and Internet marketing strategies, our clients benefit from increased recognition, improved branding, and accelerated lead generation and profitability within the social media space. We utilize a diverse range of Web 2.0 sites to build links, traffic, and authority.

(Remember, whoever gets the most mindshare wins.)

Contact info:

www.mindsharecorp.com/rachna@mindsharecorp.com

Disruptive Excellence

Getting Ahead in a Down Market

Ray Cronise

Sales and marketing are constantly reinforcing the idea of product or company differentiation. What are your unique selling positions? What are your competition's offerings? Why does your product cost more? Let's face the facts—when the market is down, it is very easy for your product to become a commodity product, because it is a common sales myth that in the end it's *always about price.*

Nothing could be further from the truth if you are value selling. When the market is sliding and management is clamoring for any sales, you must avoid the commodity product trap.

Just remember that if Rolex ever decides it is selling a device to simply tell time, then there is no reason to choose a Rolex over a Casio. Should the Rolex sales force enter the "time-telling" business, they will be doomed. Selling on price is not selling at all; it is order taking. If you are in the order-taking business, especially in a down market, your product or service is always subject competitive price slashing, which will eliminate *you* as competition. There will always be someone who comes along as a startup or runs their business more like a hobby and who is willing to cut corners to cut price. There are times when reducing price can be a sound competitive strategy, but it has to be part of a disruptive innovation that simultaneously cuts the cost of manufacturing the product or delivering the service. More often sales will miss the most important opportunity in the sales tool chest: innovations that move the product or service to a new set of customers who have a different value base. The reason is because these innovations may in fact be contrary to your current customer demands.

LISTENING TO YOUR CUSTOMERS CAN KILL YOUR COMPANY

A disruptive technology, or innovation, is defined by a product or service that may significantly lower the cost of a product but, more important, introduces a different set of attributes than those valued by current mainstream customers. In effect, disruptive technologies grow new markets and customers by introducing products or services that current customers are unwilling or hesitant to use. Clayton M. Christensen and Joseph L. Bower introduced the term *disruptive technology* in a 1995 article in the *Harvard Business Review*.[1] They described many examples of companies that ultimately failed because of failure to embrace disruptive innovations, and the market moved on and left them behind.

---

[1]*Disruptive Technologies: Catching the Wave*, J. L. Bower and C. M. Christensen, *Harvard Business Review*, January–February 1995.

Hard drives are everywhere today, and the new economic benchmark is the price per gigabyte (GB). When Christensen's article was authored in 1995, hard drives were priced by cost per *megabyte* (1000 MB = 1 GB). Between 1976 and 1992 hard drive prices dropped from US$560 to $5 per MB. In early 2009 hard drives can be purchased for about 10 cents per *gigabyte,* and prices will continue to fall. The most amazing part of this entire technological revolution is that *not one of the independent disk-drive manufacturers that existed in 1976 survived until 1995.* In fact, all these companies failed because they listened only to their existing customers and, in satisfying the products and services these customers needed at that time, ignored the very innovations that eventually put them out of business. By the time they realized where the market had moved, it was too late to catch up.

Certainly you cannot completely ignore your current customers, but failure to embrace key points of product differentiation with an open willingness to do things differently than your competition could be your biggest mistake. Always remember that selling value will involve differentiation, and the root word of differentiation is *different.* Every great salesperson must avoid chasing competitive features, but more important, you must embrace and promote the elements of your product, service, or company that are different from those of your competition. It is an ironic twist that though the sales force is always asking how their product or service is different from the competition, terror can ensue from an innovation or marketing message that goes counter to what current customers are demanding. Innovations are not just limited to new technology; they can also include how the product is competitively positioned in the market.

It is important to recognize that how the market perceives you and your product directly affects your ability to not only differentiate but build value and move you out of commodity order taking. There is nothing more critical in a down market.

It is the easiest time for your company to allow R&D to become "rip-off and duplicate" and to let price be the single most important differentiation. In a down market, becoming a commodity product or service can allow short-term sales boosts to become long-term company failure. Just ask any of those hard drive manufacturers that were first to market in 1976. This message will start with your personal relationship with your current customers; sell yourself first. It must not stop there; you have to sell your product while avoiding order taking at all costs.

THERE'S NO "I" IN TEAM

So, what can you do to help your company better position itself? How can you be part of the disruptive innovation solution? The key is to always think *disruptive excellence*. How can *you* excel with your product or service? What are the best features of your company? How can you challenge the status quo in your industry? Are you perceived as industry experts? In earlier chapters, we discussed the importance of blogs and personal web sites in achieving a personal positioning and recognition. There may not be any "I" in team, but don't fool yourself, there is an "I" in failure, and you should make sure that "I" isn't *you*. Teamwork can in fact be antithetical to success. At one time or another we have all bemoaned that "design by committee" just doesn't work. Many times the sales force's fear of market rejection on first introduction of new ideas is the very impediment to corporate differentiation and success.

> "A camel is a horse designed by committee."
> —Sir Alec Issigonis

You are the front line for your company, and while keeping within the overall message and brand, your job is ultimately to sell what the company has created. Having something different to offer in a down market gets you noticed. Once noticed, you will *succeed* by understanding and overcoming market objections. Don't allow your initial customer rejections or the rejections of a few to dominate your thought process and dampen your enthusiasm. Most, if not all, great innovations are rejected on first introduction. Burt Rutan, arguably one of the most innovative aeronautical engineers of the past 50 years, says, "You have to have confidence in nonsense if you want to innovate. An innovation is by definition something that half of the people think is *impossible*, and half say, well, maybe it can be done." Rutan knows innovation—he was the first to fly around the world nonstop without refueling. He was first to launch a privately funded spaceship, winning the $10 million Ansari X Prize. Now he has joined forces with billionaire entrepreneur Richard Branson to build the first private suborbital spaceship for Virgin Galactic's launch into space tourism. His very success in all these projects was a result of breaking all the rules and letting his goals define his approach.

What drives innovators like Rutan and Branson is a dedicated persistence to success in spite of initial failures or rejections. In a down market you must have the same tenacity, persistence, and preparation to tower above the competition and be noticed. Your presentations must be rehearsed and refined; don't leave them to chance. Make recordings of what you are saying and then go back to listen and watch your sales presentation. At first you will find it very unnerving to hear your voice and see yourself, but don't let this stop you; it is very common for the most seasoned public speaker to cringe when he sees himself on video. You will learn and you will improve by going through this process.

This is where you will learn the most about the "I" in your team. Once all the brochures are printed, the web site published, and the product priced, can you do your part and sell it? Too often sales blames their own failure to properly prepare for and enthusiastically embrace a product or marketing message on the very innovative and differentiated message that can put them ahead of the competition. If you find yourself looking to the competition for all the good ideas and innovations, perhaps you are working for the wrong company. On the other hand, if you can't seem to overcome objection in the marketplace for a differentiated product or service, it may be your lack of preparation or persistence that is the true issue.

WHAT EVERY SCIENTIST KNOWS ABOUT FAILURE IS YOUR SECRET TO SUCCESS

Behind all the stereotypes of lab coats, taped up glasses, and pocket protectors is one salient characteristic that makes great scientists: They understand that the only time they learn something is when they are wrong. In fact, many scientists are accused of always thinking they are right. I always find this odd because I can't imagine someone going around in life saying things they believe to be untrue—of course they always think they are right. In fact, the paradox is that great scientists actually embrace being wrong because they know that new things are learned only when they are wrong. Success more often comes after a long succession of repeated failures, and this is where persistence pays. It's also a secret weapon to kill the competition.

In a down market, it is extremely important to turn the popular belief of success versus failure on its head. If you see success in one direction and failure in the other direction, you are missing a critical key to increase your odds of succeeding. Instead of this push-me/pull-me mindset, think of every failure as a statistical step toward success. Once you train your mind, body language, and message to smile and push forward with every rejection or failure you encounter, you will become an unstoppable sales machine. Again, I can't overemphasize preparation and rehearsal of your sales message. Once you feel you really have it down, take it to the street with an unbridled dedication to succeed. In a down market (it also works in *any* market), be prepared for failure and rejection and move past it. Every time you hear a no, register what the objection is and then see yourself one no closer to a yes. Avoid the common mistake of coming back to the company after a few rejections and whining about what the competition's saying, doing, or offering. If you are good at what you do, it is your job as a member of the team to make it work—no excuses allowed.

The underlying message is that you must not let the artificial biases of your customer or your perception force your company into the same tailspin of early hard drive manufacturers. To be a leader and have a differentiated message—to embrace disruptive excellence—is to believe in something that "half of the people think is impossible." The best part of this approach is that as it begins to work, through your proper preparation, rehearsal, and delivery of your marketing message, your competition is not going to copy you but in fact will probably think you are crazy in your approach. By the time they figure out what you are doing, you will have moved the market or created a new customer base, and they will be in the position of catching up. As your team does this repeatedly, you will slowly gain a reputation as the market innovators, the leaders, and the experts, and everyone wants to be on or a part of the winning team.

GIVE BEAN COUNTERS PLENTY OF BEANS TO COUNT

Probably one of the worst mistakes any company can make that wants to introduce disruptive excellence as a competitive edge is to allow accounting to run sales and marketing. When sales start to dwindle, it is so easy to become conservative and retreat. This is a huge mistake. The company must be fiscally responsible—cash is king in any business—but this does not mean you have to abandon an innovative and differentiated message for a more conservative approach. Here is an actual quote from a memo concerning a corporate reorganization, separating sales from the marketing message as the sales began to fall due to a slowing economy:

> You will continue to be in charge of Marketing and as such you will be responsible for identifying and crafting the Sales Message along with the necessary tools to communicate that message. You will also be expected to work cooperatively with the Sales Team to ensure that all measures are being considered and necessarily implemented to maximize our ability to sell product. Final approval regarding the Sales Message and the tools that will be created and disseminated to further the success of the message, will be given by a majority vote of the Board of Directors.

Did they make camels at this company? This is the kind of corporate jabberwocky that all too often creeps into our everyday decisions. One of the greatest mistakes spawned by an insatiable drive for "teamwork" is to allow the organizational chart to rule the world. In an honest effort at open communications and corporate-wide "buy-in," we often create task forces and groups that end up designing camels. The result is *paralysis by analysis* and mediocrity is the end product; this does not make for good innovation or differentiation. Keep teams lean until the product or sales message has had enough time to mature. The idea is not to create secret societies and covert operations; rather, you want to keep the innovative team lean. In the case of sales, this is exactly why the emphasis was placed on *you* in Chapter 2. It is your job to sell yourself first, and then it is equally important to sell what your company is offering.

Want a great example to show your management or employees, to take the sting out of you pointing out this sort of organizational insanity? Go to YouTube.com and search "Designing the Stop Sign." It's a great example of what *not* to do if you want disruptive excellence to infect your company. Remember, it's okay if you aren't at the forefront of innovation and ideas; after all, your responsibility to the company is to *sell* them. If you want to create your own personal value, then become the organization's resident "can sell ice to an Eskimo" guy and be on the forefront of new product adoption and creating new markets. On the other hand, if you never get selected to participate in a new product launch, look in the mirror—perhaps you don't embrace or project the attitude that breeds confidence and success for new ventures. It's okay, though, because this sort of skill can be learned through tenacity, persistence, and preparation. Attitude is infectious, and if you are perceived as a sales team member who embraces new ideas and deals well with initial market failures and rejections, your inbox will be bursting with opportunity.

CREATIVE CORRUPTION AND BLIND CREATIVE COLLECTIVISM

There is a saying in the intelligence community that rings true for every organization: *E-mail is forever*. Once you send an e-mail, you're never going to get it back. Furthermore, a smooth-running, perfectly innovative project can be derailed in the few milliseconds it takes to press the Enter key. Think about the people you copy on the distribution list and why you want them to be there. Equally important for those who receive informational cc/bcc e-mails, think before you react. Your role in an organizational chart does not automatically mean that your opinion is necessarily going to help an innovative product launch. At the early stages of any innovative development, take a lesson from the playbook of the most productive innovators and don't allow *anyone* on your team who believes the new idea is impossible. Even if they doubt it, keep them away.

Remember aeronautical engineer Burt Rutan? It's a cast-in-stone rule in his organization that if you don't believe it can be done, not only are you not on the team working on it, you don't get any progress reports or knowledge of it in the first place. There will be plenty of time to input and massage the product or message after it is ready to be refined. During the early development stage the goal is to move fast, break it, and fix it. If an innovation by definition is something that "half the people think is *impossible*," then that half has a vested interest in the project failing. Most people find it far more appealing to be right than to learn from being wrong. Equally important is the fact that each time you add a new person to the cc/bcc, the project is going to be slowed while everyone responds to help this person catch up. Add to that human nature of inclusivity and wanting to put your thumbprint on the project and you end up with the cliché example of putting nine women on a pregnancy to get it done in a month. Some projects just take time, and creating the right lean team in the beginning and sticking to it until you're ready to expand is the fastest way to get a product or new message to the marketplace. Don't let your organizational chart kill creativity in your workforce; create lean teams for any innovative product or marketing message development.

WHEN EVERYBODY'S SPECIAL, NOBODY IS SPECIAL

This line was used twice in the Pixar superhero movie *The Incredibles* in relation to the family's superpowers and a societal quest to find the "best" in everyone. It's a mistake to let "fitting in" trump the idea of being best. In sales, you want to positively portray personal and corporate success, and this is especially important when markets are down. Disruptive excellence is an attitude, not always a process. There are many different ways that new, disruptive innovations and marketing messages come into existence. As a sales team, our job is to embrace these new ideas and develop new customers for our company. When possible we also need to convert new customers and move them into a market space that leaves the competition behind. Being different and standing out are a key litmus test to gauge how your company is doing in creating value.

Disruptive Excellence Top-Ten List:

1. Learn and sell value at every opportunity.
2. Rehearse, rehearse, rehearse your sales message.
3. See failure as a step to success.
4. Create excellence at all levels of your company.
5. Don't quit on first rejection; most great ideas are initially rejected.
6. Become industry resources and experts.
7. Break it fast and fix it; avoid paralysis by analysis.
8. Challenge the status quo.
9. Keep innovative teams to minimum contribution levels; don't let organizational charts rule the roster, and use cc/bcc sparingly.
10. New customers and markets are everywhere; don't allow current customers to kill innovative new ideas and markets.

Being different doesn't guarantee success, but being the same is positively a guarantee of nondifferentiation. There is no substitute for rehearsing your sales message and making sure that you can overcome rejections. You don't want to become a statistical failure, like the innovative early hard drive manufacturers that let today's customers and markets rob tomorrow's new opportunity. Every successful sales team member must find ways to be seen in the industry as embracing new thought and ideas while promoting those in the company that are truly industry experts. Not everyone is going to be "special" in the same way, but your ability to stand out is limited only by your dedication to becoming excellent at what you do every day.

Ray Cronise is the founder of Disruptive Excellence, a consulting firm specializing in injecting disruptive innovation into company product lines or markets to achieve unprecedented competitive edge and revenue growth (www.DisruptiveExcellence.com). Ray served as a material scientist for 15 years at NASA's Marshall Space Flight Center, where he worked on various microgravity material science payloads for the Space Shuttle and Spacelab missions. In 1993 he was a co-founder of Zero Gravity Corporation (www.gozerog.com), which was the first company to offer FAA-approved weightless parabolic flights for fun and entertainment.

His undergraduate and graduate studies were in chemistry, and in 1988 he was among 104 students from 21 nations who were selected to attend the inaugural session of the International Space University at the Massachusetts Institute of Technology. Ray has authored over 30 peer-reviewed scientific studies and numerous composite/pool industry trade publications and holds several patents. He can be contacted at raycronise@gmail.com.

Ray would like to dedicate this chapter to his mentor, dear friend, and defender of excellence through education, Konrad Dannenberg, who passed away at 96 years old the day after this writing was completed. Konrad was a member of the original German rocket scientist team that put man on the moon and was a constant source of inspiration during their 27 year friendship. He will be dearly missed.

How to Effectively Use Facebook to Find Your Ideal Work, Build Your Brand, and Increase Your Sales

Mari Smith

WHAT IS FACEBOOK?

Facebook.com refers to itself as a "social utility." Essentially, it is a membership platform on the Internet where you can network with fellow members.

Founded in February 2004, Facebook is a social utility that
helps people communicate more efficiently with their friends,
family and coworkers. The company develops technologies that
facilitate the sharing of information through the social graph,
the digital mapping of people's real-world social connections.
Anyone can sign up for Facebook and interact with the people
they know in a trusted environment.[1]

I like to think of Facebook as a relationship management
tool. Facebook allows me to manage two types of relationships:
(1) those individuals I know already, such as personal friends,
family members, distant relations, and people I went to school
with, and (2) people I do not yet know personally but would
like to, such as other experts in my industry, authors, speakers,
media contacts—even celebrities.

Of the hundreds of social networks on the Internet today,
Facebook is one of the few that rigorously enforces its terms
of use. The site allows one account per person that has to be
in your real first and last name. Accounts set up in business
names, fake names, or duplicate accounts will be deactivated—
sooner or later.

You can have up to 5000 friends on your personal account
(Profile), but if you try to grow your network of friends "too
fast" or write too many wall posts, send too many e-mails, or
post too many links, you may well trigger one of Facebook's
bots and have your account deactivated.

Though your main account is deemed personal, I highly
recommend that you choose to utilize your personal Profile for
predominantly business purposes. The primary reason for this
is the power of Facebook's news feed, where the aggregate of
all your friends' activities shows up in your feed, and vice versa.
I'll explain further in this chapter.

---

[1] Source: www.facebook.com/press/info.php?factsheet.

WHY FACEBOOK?

Whether you choose to have a personal Profile or not, you can also have a powerful representation of your business by setting up a Facebook page, often referred to as a *fan page* or *business page*. On these pages, you have "fans" (the political pages have "supporters"). The good news is that you can have an *unlimited number* of fans, you can message them all at once, and your page gets indexed by Google!

There are many reasons that you should tap into the power of this social networking giant for business and career-building purposes. Here are my top five reasons to be active on Facebook for business purposes:

1. Size and rate of growth
2. Demographic
3. Market research
4. Search engine optimization
5. Targeted ad campaigns

Social networks are now used by 26 percent of Internet users, up from 17 percent in 2006.[2] Facebook is the number-one online social network; it had well over 150 million active members as of February 2009. For some time, analysts have been predicting Facebook's size to be at 500 million members by 2011, but at its current growth rate, Facebook will reach that half-billion-member mark much sooner than 2011. Facebook is a robust platform, focused intently on growth and dominating the social networking arena. It's doing a fine job so far.

Contrary to popular belief that Facebook is "just for kids," the average age of Facebook users is 35. Its fastest-growing demographic is 30-year-olds. Facebook's users are young, but

---

[2] Source: eMarketer, www.emarketer.com/Article.aspx?id=1006892.

they're not all teenagers or in their early twenties. Studies show that more members on Facebook have college degrees than on the likes of MySpace.

Through your own Facebook (fan) page, Facebook Group, social ads, and the advanced profile search, you can conduct highly useful and accurate market research. Even being a "fly on the wall" by observing and charting the day-to-day activities of your Facebook friends can yield terrific insights for marketing purposes.

Facebook business pages are indexed by Google, allowing you to have significant search engine positioning when your page is set up correctly and generates regular activity. My own Facebook page is often number one on Google for the search term "buzz marketing specialist."

Facebook's social ads are somewhat similar to Google AdWords insofar as you purchase ads for specific demographics for impressions or clicks. That means that your ad will only show up on the profiles of members who match the criteria you select. The "social" part of the ad is where you advertise a page, group, or event inside Facebook, and you have the option to include social actions (which I highly recommend you do). Then when a Facebook member interacts with the ad, her avatar and name may be "bolted on" to your ad—thus essentially endorsing your ad to that member's own network of friends.

HOW TO GET PROSPECTS TO BEAT A PATH TO YOUR DOOR

You may recall the concept that if you "build a better mousetrap, the world will beat a path to your door." This is no longer the case. You could be sitting in your office with the most incredible mousetrap in the world... and scarcely enough people would know about it for you to run a profitable business or to hire you.

Here's what I recommend: Instead of focusing on the mousetrap, you focus on the path by creating what I call *radical strategic visibility*. That is, you're seen in all the right places by all the right people at all the right times. In fact, your friends and colleagues say to you with joy in their voice, "John, I keep seeing you everywhere! You're all over the place."

With the right type of regular activity, you leave your "footprints" (or drop "breadcrumbs") all around Facebook and beyond such that the right people are automatically attracted to you. They feel drawn to follow your path to then see what your mousetrap is all about. This is the difference between attraction marketing and push marketing. And this applies whether you're in business for yourself, you work for a company, or you're seeking employment.

Now, the key to this radical strategic visibility is that you are seen to have *focus!* You want to have people see your activities with consistency, congruence, transparency, and authenticity.

My general rule of thumb for posting anything on Facebook (or anywhere online, for that matter)—whether text, audio, video, or photos—is, "Would I be comfortable if this showed up on the front page of the *New York Times* or in a Google search?" and/or "Would I be proud for my grandchildren to see this in a few decades' time?"

So, I recommend that all your activities on Facebook be deliberate and strategic. Everything you do should be about building brand awareness—even if that brand is you as a person. By using your (personal) Profile for business purposes, part of your strategy may be to build a network of up to 5000 specifically chosen individuals who are a mix of (a) your target market, (b) potential strategic alliances who can help you increase your business, and (c) your personal friends and family.

I'm often asked about privacy and how to keep your personal life personal. The thing is, with the popularity of Web 2.0 and online social networks, the lines between professional and personal are very blurry. However, you don't have to live in a glass house. It's important that you draw a line in the sand and decide what is *private*. You'll find further reading on this topic at this blog post: http://whyfacebook.com/2008/02/08/facebook-personal-professional-and-private/.

THIRTY WAYS TO CREATE VISIBILITY

Earlier I mentioned the power of Facebook's news feed. Every action you take on Facebook creates what they call a *story*, and that story is pushed out into your mini-feed (the main section of your own Profile) and into the news feed of your friends. So, the more (hand-picked) friends you have, the more radical strategic visibility you can create.

I created a video on how to use Facebook in five minutes a day, which you can see here: http://snipurl.com/facebook5mins. To accelerate your visibility when you're in growth mode, here are 30 ways to create visibility:

1. Update your status.
2. Comment on your friends' status.
3. Upload photos.
4. Tag photos.
5. Comment on photos.
6. Upload videos.
7. Tag videos.
8. Comment on videos.
9. Write notes.
10. Import your blog into notes.
11. Tag people mentioned in notes.
12. Comment on notes.
13. Share links with posted items.
14. Comment on others' posted items.
15. Join groups.
16. Create your own group.

17. Write on the wall of groups.
18. Upload photos, videos, links to groups.
19. Write on the discussion board of groups.
20. RSVP yes for events.
21. Write on the wall of events.
22. Upload photos, videos, and links to events.
23. Become a fan of a fan page.
24. Write on the wall of a fan page.
25. Write a review of a fan page.
26. Write a review of an app.
27. Interact with the six types of ads. (See this post: http://snipurl.com/fb6ads.)
28. Use the Share button.
29. Install apps.
30. Interact with apps.

HOW TO RECRUIT TOP SALES STAFF USING FACEBOOK

If you're headhunting for a specific hire for your company, there are many ways to use Facebook to identify potential candidates, including direct keyword search, joining and viewing groups, advanced profile search, and placing ads.

In direct keyword search, the master search bar in the top right of Facebook's blue navigation bar searches the entire Facebook site for people, pages, groups, events, applications, and now the entire Web via Windows Live Search. So, for example, say you're looking for software sales staff; just by entering the term "software sales" in the search box, then clicking the tab for People, you'll see a number of Facebook member profiles that match this keyword search.

In addition, look at groups that you could join and/or observe members to make direct contact with potential candidates.

(*Note:* You can contact Facebook members via e-mail without necessarily adding them as friends.)

There is also a more advanced search feature inside Facebook that isn't that obvious; the easiest way to find it is via this direct URL: www.facebook.com/advanced.php. This brings up a form with all the fields of Facebook profiles and allows you to drill down and do targeted keyword searches. The one drawback is that the search is only conducted among your existing friends and the networks you belong to. This can certainly be useful if you're looking to hire a local person.

By choosing specific demographics, you could place a very targeted ad to attract qualified candidates.

FINDING NEW SOURCES OF EMPLOYMENT IN THE REPUTATION AGE

If you've been downsized out of a job or you're seeking alternative employment, establishing a strong presence on Facebook can serve your career well. Make sure you have a clean, professional Profile. Refrain from posting *any* content that could be misconstrued or that doesn't add to your overall professional image. I typically recommend sharing your private family photos, for example, via an alternative medium.

Immediately under the photo on your Facebook Profile there is a place to write free text. Write a short bio here and include the fact that you're currently seeking a position in *X* type of company. Also install the Profile HTML application that allows you to paste in your own HTML, such as an image and/or text. Essentially this is your own space to advertise the fact that you're seeking a certain type of employment. Include the way(s) you want to be contacted. The direct link to the Profile HTML app is http://apps.facebook.com/profile_html/.

One of the most read fields on Facebook Profiles is the Status Update; this is where you say what you're doing in about

160 characters. You can choose to talk about yourself in third person or first person—it's up to you. (I tend to use a mix of both, but since I'm very active on Twitter, where I only ever talk in first person, I tend to use first person more on Facebook, too.) I recommend using the Status Update field to reach out to your network of friends and share your progress with your job hunt, asking them for referrals, support, suggestions, and introductions.

Maintain a consistent, focused presence. Even in just five minutes a day, by choosing the right strategic activities and reaching out to connect with key influencers who can support you in your search, you can yield positive results in a short amount of time.

Expand your social networking to include the other two powerful social networking platforms, LinkedIn.com and Twitter.com. Be sure to have a consistent look and feel to your profile pages across multiple platforms.

SETTING UP YOUR OWN USER GROUP

Facebook groups are a powerful way to create your own focus, study, discussion, or market research group, and more. One of the primary reasons to have your own Facebook group (in addition to joining others' groups) is the fact that you can message all group members, up to 5000. This is the closest tool to having your own opt-in list; essentially your group members put up their hands and said, "Yes, I'm interested, tell me more." As the group owner, all messages you send go directly into the inbox of your members. Keep your messages short, relevant, and interesting. Don't over-message or people will leave your group.

One good use of a Facebook group comes into play when you're writing a book. You can gather interested, targeted readers and get feedback from them on chapters and book cover designs, garner testimonials, and more. Then, when your book is published, you have already established a fan base to help spread the word.

Because Facebook groups are so prolific, you'll want to adopt strategies for "stickiness"—that is, reasons for your members to keep coming back. Creating stimulating discussion topics and messaging members is one such strategy. Also, offer contests, drawings, and polls, and have your members upload content of their own. All this activity helps create more visibility for your group.

EVERYONE IN BUSINESS NEEDS AT LEAST ONE FACEBOOK PAGE

Facebook offers a feature specifically for businesses to grow their presence and increase visibility without having to have a personal account. That feature is a Facebook page, often referred to as a *fan page* or *business page*. Whereas on your personal Profile you have *friends* (limited to 5000), on a Facebook page you have *fans*, and they can be unlimited in number. You can also message all fans all at once or even target messages by certain demographics. This feature is ideal for localized events, for example.

Unlike Facebook (personal) Profiles, you can have multiple Facebook pages. So, if you have different divisions in your company or a variety of products, for example, you might create a page for each one, thus providing more search engine optimization (SEO) and visibility. Once you've created your page(s), use the Page Manager app to edit: www.facebook.com/pages/manage/.

CASE STUDY: TWO HUNDRED PERCENT GROWTH

Aboveground Realty is a six-person realty group that rents luxury lofts in Manhattan, priced between $6500 and $8500 per month. The staff needed to reach their primary target market of investment bankers and lawyers. None of their print ads were working; business dribbled in, and most people could not afford the rent prices.

A word-of-mouth marketing and social media marketing firm, theKbuzz, created a Facebook fan page for Aboveground Realty and set out to recruit fans by placing Facebook social ads linking to the company's Facebook fan page. The ads targeted employees in specific law firms, investment banks, and C-level executives and executive directors in the New York City market.

Aboveground built its fan base to over 200 of its target audience. The staff then began to communicate with each and every fan, offering free advice about renting in the New York market. By the end of 2008, Aboveground's business had increased 200 percent. When the banking industry started to falter, Aboveground's relationships formed on Facebook helped them leverage the relationships within the firms to help displaced brokers relocate and survivors of the collapse to rent bigger, better spaces.

Case study source: Caroline Kerpen, Vice President, New Buzzness Development, theKbuzz, www.thekbuzz.com.

SPECIFIC ACTION STEPS TO TAKE NOW!

1. If you haven't already done so, set up an account in your own name at Facebook.com.
   a. Upload a professional photo. It doesn't have to be too formal. In fact, a more relaxed, informal photo is ideal, though ideally one taken by a professional.
   b. Add content such as your contact information, interests, and background.
   c. If you write a blog, import your posts via the Facebook Notes application (www.facebook.com/notes.php) as well as the third-party app, Networked Blogs (http://apps.facebook.com/blognetworks/index.php).

d. Import your address book from your e-mail system to invite people you already know to be your Facebook friends.

e. Search Facebook for people you know, or would like to know, and add them as friends. However, be very careful not to add too many friends at once; I recommend sending no more than about 20 outgoing friend requests per day.

f. Include your Facebook profile link in your e-mail signature file, business cards, blogs, and so on, to encourage people to request to be your friend (incoming requests). To find your Profile link, mouse over your name in the top blue navigation bar; that's your Profile URL. You can shorten your URL in one of these ways: (a) with this app: http://apps.facebook.com/webaddress/, or (b) create your own redirect link, such as http://marismith.com/facebook, or (c) buy a domain such as *yourname*onfacebook.com and forward it to your Facebook profile URL.

g. Engage in regular activity, as mentioned in the Thirty Ways to Create Visibility list.

2. Set up at least one Facebook business (fan) page to represent your business. Here's how: Click the Advertising link at the foot of any Facebook.com Web page, whether you have a personal profile or not, then click Pages. Or use the direct link: www.facebook.com/pages/create.php.

a. Build out the basic content plus add the Facebook MarkUp Language (FBML) app. You can have as many installations of this app as you like, and paste in rich media—HTML, images, and video. To find the FBML app, simply enter *fbml* in the master search bar and look for the app called Static FBML.

b. Experiment with a series of Facebook social ads. Click the Advertising link at the foot of any Facebook.com Web page, whether you have a personal profile or not, then click Create an Ad. Drive viewers of your ad back to your Facebook page.

In summary, keep in mind that you want to incorporate Facebook as part of your *overall* marketing strategy, not as your only focus. Furthermore, whether you run your own business, you're an independent professional, or you work for a company and/or are looking for a new career, Facebook offers a powerful array of features to support you objectives.

Dubbed the Pied Piper of Facebook by FastCompany.com, **Mari Smith** is a relationship marketing specialist and social media business coach. She helps entrepreneurs, business owners, and independent professionals accelerate their profits using an integrated social marketing strategy, with particular focus on Facebook and Twitter. Mari is passionate about showing fellow professionals how to develop powerful profitable relationships.

Find out more about Mari Smith and her products and services on her two blogs:

http://marismith.com
http://whyfacebook.com

How to Sell Real Estate in a Tough Market and Grow Your Business Year after Year at the Same Time

Craig Ernst

At this point, it's not news to anyone that the real estate gold rush is over, at least for now and at least for most folks. But as a professional real estate agent, is it really over for you, or is it possible that it's just getting started?

Even though many agents who were previously doing well are now struggling and many have dropped out of the business entirely (with more disappearing every time MLS and board renewals come up), there are small numbers of agents out there who are having their best years ever. Skeptical? It's true, but it doesn't happen by accident.

How are these "lucky" agents doing so well?

When I speak to agents all around the country, the ones who are inevitably doing best in these challenging times are agents who have two things: They have a strong database, consisting of past clients, their sphere of influence, and, perhaps, the residents of one or more geographical farms, and they have a strong system for staying in regular contact with that database of past and potential clients.

In effect, agents with these strong databases have "fenced in" a portion of the market, and they draw to themselves a significant portion of the business that arises from that group on an ongoing basis. And of course, no matter the market conditions, real estate is always being bought and sold.

Before we get started talking about the specific things we can do to get more clients and more closings, there are a couple of things that I should point out that these trend-bucking agents know that other agents either don't know or don't understand the importance of.

SALIENT FACT NUMBER ONE: THE BUYING AND SELLING OF REAL ESTATE IS PRIMARILY DRIVEN BY LIFE EVENTS

Although major changes in the financial markets and in our national or local economies can and will affect the total number of real estate transactions at any given time, it's the life events of individual consumers that are the real underlying drivers of demand in the marketplace.

People will get married, and people will get divorced. New babies are born, and old folks pass away. Some people receive promotions and transfers to a new city, and some people lose their jobs or become disabled and unable to work. These are just a sampling of the types of life events that often prompt the purchase or sale of real estate. So, no matter what happens in terms of the overall marketplace, real estate will always change hands in sufficient quantities for you to make a good (or even an exceptional) living as a real estate professional. Notice that I said there will always be enough business for *you* to do well, not for all agents to do well.

SALIENT FACT NUMBER TWO: REAL ESTATE AGENTS SHOULD POSITION THEMSELVES AS KNOWLEDGEABLE AND TRUSTWORTHY ADVISORS

It's no secret that most people prefer to do business with people they know, like, and trust. And if they don't know anyone personally who fits the bill, they often rely on friends, family, and neighbors to recommend someone *they* know, like, and trust.

What Kind of Effect Does This Have on the Business of Individual Agents?

According to the National Association of Realtors®, over 50 percent of all home buyers chose their agents based on the fact that they had either used them before or that they were recommended to them by friends, neighbors, or relatives. For sellers, that number was over 70 percent.

What this means is that under any type of market conditions, somewhere upward of 60 percent of the transactions in the marketplace are being conducted by agents who acquired their clients through some sort of personal connection. And in many of those situations, the clients were very likely acquired in a noncompetitive environment (that is, without having to compete directly with another agent for the business).

How Can Agents Capitalize on These Salient Facts?

So, the question is, how will these "salient facts" help *you* generate more clients and more closings?

The good news is that most prospective clients already have some motivation to buy or sell property before they ever speak to us. So, unlike sales professionals in many other industries, real estate pros don't primarily increase business by creating new needs and desires in consumers.

Rather, we should work at trying to be a visible and valuable resource so that when those inevitable life events come about, we're there to be of service and to be part of the process. This is sometimes called *putting yourself in front of business*.

There are two ways that agents can put themselves in front of more business. One is to expand the number of people out there who know you (or feel that they do), who like you, and who trust you. The other is to deepen the relationships with people who already see you in the aforementioned light.

The good news is that you don't need to schedule a bunch of candlelight dinners to deepen those existing relationships! Psychological research has shown that simple repetitive contact between people often increases feelings of "liking" in each of them, all other things being equal. So, by staying in contact frequently through a variety of means, you can achieve this increased "liking" effect, not to mention being more "front of mind."

There are a number of books, courses, and live training programs out there (real estate specific and otherwise) about how to cultivate more direct business and referrals through a system of both personal contacts and more marketing-oriented contacts (client or neighborhood newsletters, for instance). For that reason and for reasons of space, I won't go into detail about that aspect here.

But I would like to share with you some very specific strategies that you can implement now to help expand the number of people you have in your database—strategies that you likely won't find anyone else sharing with you in detail.

Before I start in on those specifics, though, I should reiterate the differences between personal prospecting and marketing. Prospecting and marketing are two sides of the same coin, and ideally your client acquisition plan should include some of each. Prospecting usually involves you personally seeking out business or personally providing some type of value now in hopes of future business or referrals, whereas marketing involves the use of some mass medium (newspapers, direct mail, the Web, and the like) to reach many people at once.

Here I focus on personal prospecting, not marketing, for a couple of reasons. First, this is a book on selling, not marketing (and personal prospecting is a form of selling). Second, marketing is most appropriate when you have more money than time; prospecting is most appropriate when you have more time than money. I think that these days most agents fall into the latter category. Prospecting gives you a chance to put some "sweat equity" into your business. (If you'd like to read about real estate marketing, you can find a good many free articles on the subject at my blog, http://RealEstateSuccessPath.com.)

How to Quickly Build Yourself a Massive Potential Client Database

There are several ways I can think of that an agent might quickly, cost effectively, and systematically build a valuable database of potential clients and referral sources. But we don't have a whole book to go over all those! So, I'm going to give you a detailed example of what I think is the absolute easiest way to go about this task. And with the detailed script I'm going to give you, you can get started this very weekend, if you like.

The method I detail below is called *geographic prospecting*— a type of up-close-and-personal (and very cost-effective) geographical farming.

One of the most tried-and-true methods of marketing for new clients is geographical farming. Geo-farming is most often a marketing-oriented activity that usually requires a fairly substantial budget and a long-tern commitment in order to be successful.

However, geographic prospecting can be done either solo or in conjunction with geo-farming and typically yields quicker results, with a minimal financial expenditure.

Remember, our goal here is to quickly build a database of potential clients and referrers that we can keep in contact with and that will bring us business on an ongoing basis. The surest way to do this is to target a desirable group (pick an in-demand neighborhood), introduce yourself to that group, and bring something valuable to the table so that they will want to hear from you again.

And yes, I am talking about actually walking a neighborhood, knocking on some doors, and meeting people. Now, this probably sounds a bit scary, but I am going to make this so drop-dead easy for you, you'll wonder why you never did it before.

So, How—*Specifically*—Do We Do This?

GEOGRAPHICAL PROSPECTING

Step 1. Choose a neighborhood.

Step 2. Prepare an offer.

Step 3. Prepare a script.

Step 4. Go to work and start making contacts.

Step 5. Follow up and profit.

Step One: Choose a Neighborhood

There's all kinds of analysis you can do to pick the absolutely optimal neighborhood for your geographic prospecting, but the neighborhood doesn't have to be statistically ideal. A couple of things, though: It should be a neighborhood that's reasonably popular and desirable (a neighborhood that you can get excited about), and it should be a neighborhood that has a good amount of yearly movement (that is, a healthy number of sales each year). Usually an area with homes priced in the upper-middle portion of your market will work just fine. Also, anything over 1000 homes is probably way too big. In fact, for your first neighborhood I'd pick something about half that or smaller, so about 500 or fewer homes.

Step Two: Prepare an Offer

In today's hyperkinetic world, people will not give you the pro-verbial time of day unless you can offer them something of value in exchange for their time and attention. Luckily, there are two things that are always true about homeowners: They're always interested in what their home is worth, and they're always interested in what their neighbors' homes are worth! So, there are two obvious offers to make to them: Offer a free home evaluation (CMA), and offer a free list of recent sales (a market report). If you're inclined to, you can get fancy with the market report and give them lots of graphs and percentages. It's up to you. But a well-laid-out list of current homes for sale and recent sales, along with their respective list and sale prices, should work just as well.

Step Three: Prepare a Script

This is the thing that will keep most agents from ever using a system like this—the abject fear of knocking on someone's door and actually having someone answer, because . . . well, what do you *say*? Fortunately, I've solved this problem for you by offering you the battle-tested (just kidding about the battle part) script that follows.

All kidding aside, not knowing beforehand what you're going to say is the death knell of good prospecting. The following script is a guide, but you should write it on index cards and role-play it extensively with a colleague until you're comfortable with it. You can also take those index cards with you when you do your neighborhood walkthroughs. Here's the sample script:

> Hi, my name is Susan Alexander. Are you the homeowner? By the way, you'll be glad to know that I'm not selling anything, and I'm not collecting money for anyone! *{big smile}* The reason I am stopping by today is that I'm a real estate agent, and I specialize in the *{community name}* neighborhood here, and I'm putting together a new neighborhood web site to publicly promote the neighborhood and help put its best face forward. And of course, increased interest in a neighborhood often leads to increased property values. Does that make sense?
>
> Would you mind if I asked your opinion on a couple of things regarding the neighborhood? It shouldn't take long. Do you have a couple of minutes?

What types of questions should you ask? Here are some examples:

> How long have you lived in the neighborhood?
>
> Where did you live previously?
>
> How do you like things here, as compared to there?
>
> What are some of your favorite things about living here?
>
> What do you personally feel might be some of the most appealing aspects of the neighborhood for someone who's thinking about living here?
>
> Is there anything that you think the community needs to work on, something that could really be improved that would make it a better place for everyone?
>
> By the way, have you ever given any thought to selling this property?

Now, to continue with the script:

> Thanks so much for taking the time to speak with me today. I actually have a gift to leave with you as a token of my appreciation. Hopefully, it's something you'll find useful. I've

done a little market report here. It shows which homes in the neighborhood are currently for sale as well as the homes that have sold over the past few months and how much they've sold for. So, again, please accept this as a thank-you, and I hope you find it interesting.

Oh, and there's also a coupon clipped to that for a free home evaluation, so if you're ever thinking of selling, or even if you're just curious about how much your home is worth in today's market, you can just give me a call or fill out the form on my web site (or e-mail me) and I'll work up a list of comparables for you and give you an estimate of what your home's currently worth.

Last thing . . . I'm actually going to be sending out a new market report for the neighborhood every month *{or every three months, whatever you decide}*, and I was wondering if you'd be interested in those? *{Usually, this answer will be yes.}* Great. Would you mind writing down your e-mail address here and printing your name and the name of your significant other, and I'll make sure you get that update.

Thanks again. Would you mind if I stopped back by in a few months, next time I do a neighborhood walkthrough? Good deal. It was a pleasure meeting you.

Pretty simple, huh?

Here are a couple of "what-ifs" and things about the script you might be wondering about.

What if no one's home?

First thing, you'll want to pick a couple of different times to do your neighborhood walkthroughs so that you catch people with different types of schedules. In general, Saturday mornings and Sunday afternoons tend to be good. You may also want to try a weekday morning or two, to try to catch stay-at-home parents, people who work at home, or retired folks (depending on the demographics of your area).

Second, you'll want to keep a checklist of the addresses you successfully visit (those with someone home). After a couple of tries, you may want to leave a little plastic bag on the door handle containing a short introductory letter or handwritten note and the market report and home evaluation certificate you would've left in person, along with an invitation (and a method) to sign up for future market reports. Leaving a few hard candies in the bag also can't hurt.

What if they're not the homeowner?

If the kids answer the door, you'll want to ask for mom or dad. If they're not home, try back another time, or leave the plastic gift bag. If they're renters, well, I'll leave it to you to decide whether it might be productive to make contact with people who rent nice homes in nice neighborhoods!

What about this "neighborhood web site" thing?

Starting a neighborhood web site is a great idea for someone trying to network with neighborhood residents. If you have coding skills or have a webmaster, this is a no-brainer. If not, there are certain vendors that provide template-style neighborhood web sites for a modest fee. Or better yet, you can start a blog-style web site for free at sites such as Wordpress.com or Blogger.com. If you choose not to do any type of web site, the important things about the script are that you're interested in helping improve and/or promote the neighborhood and you'd like their opinion. You can have web sites developed very inexpensively at www.rentacoder.com and www.elance.com.

What if they don't want to chat or give their opinion?

That's okay. Tell them that you have a gift for them anyway (the market report and home evaluation) and see if they'd like to receive future market reports.

See? The whole thing is really pretty simple and straightforward once it's laid out.

Step Four: Go to Work and Start Making Contacts

The important thing here is to make a schedule and stick to it. I mentioned scheduling different days and times to do your walkthroughs. Dress comfortably but professionally (and wear comfortable shoes!). I'd suggest wearing your company name-tag and carrying a clipboard for your market report sign-ups. You'll be a little nervous at first, but if you can do an open house, you can do this! And remember, it's not like you're the foot-in-the-door vacuum cleaner salesman. You're a professional with information of value to offer homeowners as a gift, and you'd like to get their opinion on a few things, if they have time. That's it!

Step Five: Follow Up and Profit

Here's where it all becomes worthwhile. I'd start by sending a handwritten thank-you note to everyone I met in person. You can send a thank-you e-mail to the ones you got e-mail addresses from, but I think the handwritten notes are better all around. Of course, you will want to follow up faithfully with the market reports at whatever interval you promised. You'll also want to think of other ways to be of service and think of other items of value you can offer over time. Remember, this works really well with traditional geographic farming. Ideally, you'll want to do your full neighborhood walkthroughs two or three times a year.

Can you see how your prospecting like this can help build your database and your deal flow year after year? Believe it or not, what I've laid out for you here is just the beginning of what you can do, not only with geographic prospecting but also in terms of building up your database through face-to-face prospecting. Let your creativity be your guide. Always seek to provide value and be of service. And throw yourself right in front of all that business that's out there for the taking!

Craig Ernst is a real estate marketing strategist, a speaker, a trainer, and a writer. Craig has been professionally involved in direct selling and direct marketing since 1989 and has been active in online marketing since 1998. He invites you to visit his blog at http://RealEstateSuccessPath.com and to follow him on Twitter at http://twitter.com/CraigErnst.

BIBLIOGRAPHY

Ariely, Dan. *Predictably Irrational* (Harper Collins, 2008).

Barkow, Jerome. *The Adapted Mind: Evolutionary Psychology and the Generation of Culture* (Oxford Press, 1992).

Bell, Catherine. *Ritual Theory Ritual Practice* (Oxford University Press, 1992).

Cialdini, Robert. *The Psychology of Influence* (Collins, 2006).

Conway, Flo, and Jim Siegelman. *Snapping: America's Epidemic of Sudden Personality Change* (Stillpoint Press, 1995).

Damasio, Antonio. *The Feeling of What Happens: Body and Emotion in the Making of Consciousness* (Harvest Books, 2000).

Dillard, James Price, and Michael Pfau. *The Persuasion Handbook: Developments in Theory and Practice* (Sage Publications, Inc., 2002).

Dawkins, Richard. *The God Delusion* (Houghton Mifflin, 2006).

Gitomer, Jeffrey. *The Sales Bible: The Ultimate Sales Resource* (John Wiley & Sons, 2003).

Green, Robert. *The Art of Seduction* (Penguin, 2003).

Green, Robert. *The 33 Strategies of War* (Viking Adult, 2006).

Green, Robert. *The 48 Laws of Power* (Penguin, 2000).

Goldman, Daniel. *Social Intelligence: The New Science of Human Relationships* (Bantam, 2007).

Hawkins, David R. *Power vs. Force: The Hidden Determinants of Human Behavior* (Hay House, 2002).

Heinrichs, Jay. *Thank You for Arguing: What Aristotle, Lincoln, and Homer Simpson Can Teach Us About the Art of Persuasion* (Three Rivers Press, 2007).

Hogan, Kevin. *Covert Persuasion: Psychological Tactics and Tricks to Win the Game* (John Wiley & Sons, 2006).

Hogan, Kevin. *The Psychology of Persuasion: How to Persuade Others to Your Way of Thinking* (Pelican Publishing Company, 1996).

Kilbourne, Jean. *Can't Buy Me Love: How Advertising Changes the Way We Think and Feel* (Free Press, 2000).

Kramer, Joel, and Diane Alstad. *The Guru Papers: Masks of Authoritarian Power* (Frog LTD, 1993).

Laermer, Richard, and Mark Simmons. *Punk Marketing: Get Off Your Ass and Join the Revolution* (Collins, 2007).

Luntz, Dr. Frank. *Words That Work: It's Not What You Say, It's What People Hear* (Hyperion, 2007).

Packard, Vance. *The Hidden Persuaders* (Pocket, 1984).

Paul, John, and Deborah Micek. *Secrets of Online Persuasion: Captivating the Hearts, Minds, and Pocketbooks of Thousands Using Blogs, Podcasts, and Other New Media Marketing Tools* (Morgan James Publishing, 2006).

Pinker, Steven. *The Stuff of Thought: Language as a Window into Human Nature* (Viking Adult, 2007).

Rapaille, Clotaire. *The Culture Code: An Ingenious Way to Understand Why People Around the World Live and Buy as They Do* (Broadway, 2007).

Rumbauskas, Frank, *Never Cold Call Again* (John Wiley & Sons, 2006).

Rushkoff, Douglas. *Coercion: Why We Listen to What "They" Say* (Riverhead Trade, 2000).

Sargent, William. *Battle for the Mind: A Physiology of Conversion and Brainwashing* (Malor Books, 1997).

Sosnik, Douglas B., Matthew J. Dowd, and Ron Fournier. *Applebee's America: How Successful Political, Business, and Religious Leaders Connect with the New American Community* (Simon & Schuster, 2007).

Surowiecki, James. *The Wisdom of Crowds* (Anchor, 2005).

Underhill, Paco. *Why We Buy: The Science of Shopping* (Texere Publishing, 2001).

Williams, Roy. *The Wizard of Ads: Turning Words into Magic and Dreamers into Millionaires* (Bard Publishing, 1998).

Winn, Denise. *The Manipulated Mind: Brainwashing, Conditioning, and Indoctrination* (Malor Books, 2000).

Wiseman, Richard. *Quirkology* (Basic Books, 2007).

Zaltman, Gerald. *How Customers Think: Essential Insights into the Mind of the Market* (Harvard Business School Press, 2003).

Zinsser, William. *On Writing Well, 30th Anniversary Edition: The Classic Guide to Writing Nonfiction* (Collins, 2006).

About the Author

Dave Lakhani is the world's first Business Acceleration Strategist™ and president of Bold Approach, Inc., a business acceleration strategy firm helping companies worldwide to immediately increase their revenue through effective sales, marketing, and public relations.

Considered one of the world's top experts on the application of persuasion, Dave is in high demand and heard by corporations and trade organizations of all sizes worldwide. His advice is regularly seen in *Selling Power Magazine, Sales and Marketing Management, The Wall Street Journal, Investors Business Daily, Inc., Entrepreneur, The Today Show,* and hundreds of other media outlets. Dave is also the host of *Making Marketing Work,* a radio talk show focused on marketing strategy for growing businesses. Dave also authored *A Fighting Chance* (Prince Publishing, 1991), a section of the anthology *Ready, Aim, Hire* (Persysco, 1992), and the audio book *Making Marketing Work* (BA Books, 2004).

Dave's company, Bold Approach, Inc., was nominated as one of *FastCompany Magazine's* Fast 50 companies, and Dave was runner-up for the 2007 American Business Award for

America's Best Sales Trainer. He recently received his second nomination as America's Best Sales Trainer from the American Business Awards.

Dave is considered one of the world's top platform closers who regularly closes 20 to 70 percent of the people in the rooms he works and is often invited to speak at the largest personal development events around the world. His understanding of persuasion, sales, behavior, and human motivation make him an in-demand sales and marketing trainer and hired gun to close deals.

Dave has owned more than 10 successful businesses in the past 20 years and considers himself a serial entrepreneur and committed business builder. An avid student and lifelong learner, Dave has studied every major sales, marketing, or influence professional of the past 20 years. He's a master practitioner of neuro-linguistic programming (NLP) who has studied with NLP's founder, Richard Bandler, and is a graduate and former adjunct faculty member of the Wizard of Ads Academy.

Dave lives in Boise, Idaho, with his daughter Austria. When not on the road with clients or speaking, Dave enjoys scuba diving, skiing, martial arts, reading, and great wine.

Visit Dave online at www.BoldApproach.com.

INDEX

EXCLUSIVE FREE VIDEO TRAINING OFFER

(A $695.00 VALUE)

I'm thrilled that you made the decision to invest in your future by purchasing *How to Sell When Nobody's Buying*. I'd like to continue what you'll learn here by personally training you via video. Because you own the book, I'm going to give you a five-part personal video mentoring program on how to sell more in any economy. This training course will give you the most current information and special techniques I did not teach in the book that will show you how to dominate your marketplace.

Simply go to www.howtosellwhennobodys buying.com/video and follow the directions on the page to receive your free training video, simply for buying this book. The training is available only to buyers of this book and will transform the way you sell.